JOURNAL FOR THE STUDY OF THE OLD TESTAMENT
SUPPLEMENT SERIES
194

Sheffield Academic Press
Sheffield

Prophesying the Past

The Use of Israel's History
in the Book of Hosea

Else Kragelund Holt

Journal for the Study of the Old Testament
Supplement Series 194

Til mor og far

Copyright © 1995 Sheffield Academic Press

Published by
Sheffield Academic Press Ltd
Mansion House
19 Kingfield Road
Sheffield, S11 9AS
England

Typeset by Sheffield Academic Press
and
Printed on acid-free paper in Great Britain
by Bookcraft
Midsomer Norton, Somerset

British Library Cataloguing in Publication Data

A catalogue record for this book is available
from the British Library

ISBN 1-85075-540-X

CONTENTS

PREFACE

The present book is a revised edition of my PhD thesis, presented in June 1990 and defended in February 1991 at the Department of Old Testament studies, Faculty of Theology, University of Aarhus. While the revision and translation has taken place I have been occupied with teaching and with administrative efforts at the same Department. Therefore I have not had the opportunity to work seriously on new literature. Accordingly, only a few titles from the years 1988–94 have been added to the original manuscript.

Working with the traditio-historical questions of the book of Hosea has made me recognize the deep traditio-historical as well as literary interdependencies between the books of the Old Testament. And although the present study is rather limited in its interests (the so-called historical traditions in the book of Hosea), working on it has carried me through at least 300 years of the history of Ancient Israel. The book of Hosea clearly points towards the most productive era in the history of the Old Testament, the late exilic period.

Writing and re-writing an academic work incurs debts to many people. Without the help and encouragement from my colleagues (and friends) at the Old Testament Department I would never have started working seriously with the books of the Old Testament. First and foremost I owe gratitude to my supervisor, Professor Dr Theol. Knud Jeppesen, who in his never failing enthusiasm and love for the Old Testament has partly tempted me, partly driven me forwards. I am also indebted to the book's translator, Revd Ray Carlton Jones, PhD, Kristrup, who has done much more to the manuscript than simply translating it. For the technical problems I have received a lot of help from Mrs Birgit Winther-Hansen and Mrs Gerd Askøe at the Department's Secretariat. Aarhus University Research Foundation has supplied me with the necessary financial assistance. Finally I thank the editors of the JSOT Supplement Series for accepting the manuscript for this Series and for valuable help in the last stages of production.

The present work is not influenced by feminist theology. Nevertheless it has been made under a woman's conditions. Taking care of my children, Kasper, Morten and Marie has helped me keep my feet firmly on the ground. My husband, Revd Anders Holt, has persistently helped me to remember that two things are necessary for a theologian: believing in theology and in your own skill.

This book is dedicated to my parents, Marie and Gunnar Kragelund. Growing up in a family of songs and tales is the basic foundation for the present work.

Else Kragelund Holt
Veggerslev, August 1994

ABBREVIATIONS

AcOr	*Acta orientalia*
AOAT	Alter Orient und Altes Testament
ASTI	*Annual of the Swedish Theological Institute*
ATANT	Abhandlungen zur Theologie des Alten und Neuen Testaments
ATD	Das Alte Testament Deutsch
BDBAT	*Dielheimer Blätter zum Alten Testament*, Beiheft
Bib	*Biblica*
BKAT	Biblischer Kommentar: Altes Testament
BWANT	Beiträge zur Wissenschaft vom Alten und Neuen Testament
BZ	*Biblische Zeitschrift*
BZAW	Beihefte zur *ZAW*
CBQMS	*Catholic Biblical Quarterly* Monograph Series
ConBOT	Coniectanea biblica, Old Testament
DBAT	*Dielheimer Blätter zum Alten Testament*
DTT	*Dansk Teologisk Tidsskrift*
EvT	*Evangelische Theologie*
FRLANT	Forschungen zur Religion und Literatur des Alten und Neuen Testaments
GKB	Gesenius–Kautsch–Bergsträsser, *Hebräische Grammatik*
HK	Handkommentar zum Alten Testament
JBL	*Journal of Biblical Literature*
JETS	*Journal of the Evangelical Theological Society*
JSOTSup	*Journal for the Study of the Old Testament*, Supplement Series
KAT	Kommentar zum Alten Testament
KB	L. Koehler and W. Baumgartner (eds.), *Lexicon in Veteris Testamenti libros*
KD	*Kerygma und Dogma*
KHCAT	Kurzer Hand-Commentar zum Alten Testament
KS	Kleine Schriften
KT	Kaiser Traktate
NCB	New Century Bible
NedTT's	*Nederlands theologisch tijdschrift*
NKZ	*Neue kirchliche Zeitschrift*
OBO	Orbis biblicus et orientalis
OTL	Old Testament Library
OTS	*Oudtestamentische Studiën*
SBLDS	SBL Dissertation Series
SBU	I. Engnell (ed.), Svenskt Bibliskt Uppslagsverk, I-II
SEÅ	*Svensk Exegetisk Årsbok*

SJOT	*Scandinavian Journal of the Old Testament*
SWBA	Social World of Biblical Antiquity
SWJT	*South Western Journal of Theology*
TB	Theologische Bücherei
THAT	E. Jenni and C. Westermann (eds.), *Theologisches Handwörterbuch zum Alten Testament*
ThWAT	G.J. Botterweck and H. Ringgren (eds.), *Theologisches Wörterbuch zum Alten Testament*
TLZ	*Theologische Literaturzeitung*
TWNT	G. Kittel and G. Friedrich (eds.), *Theologisches Wörterbuch zum Neuen Testament*
TZ	*Theologische Zeitschrift*
UUÅ	Uppsala Universitets Årsskrift
VT	*Vetus Testamentun*
VTSup	*Vetus Testamentum*, Supplements
WBC	Word Biblical Commentary
WMANT	Wissenschaftliche Monographien zum Alten und Neuen Testament
ZAW	*Zeitschrift für die alttestamentliche Wissenschaft*
ZST	*Zeitschrift für systematische Theologie*
ZTK	*Zeitschrift für Theologie und Kirche*

Chapter 1

INTRODUCTION

Prefatory Remarks

During the last two decades the world of scholarship has undergone a revolution, a kind of showdown with the ruling paradigms of greater or lesser force. Examples can be found within the fields of natural and social sciences as well as within the humanities, and the tendency can be traced, too, within theology and its various disciplines, among which lies the study of the Old Testament.

Until recently, the ruling paradigm in Old Testament scholarship was dominated by German scholars such as Albrecht Alt, Gerhard von Rad and Martin Noth. Although being of different opinions, they—and many other outstanding Old Testament scholars up until our own time, the early nineties—have nevertheless been representative of a mutual belief in the human capacity thoroughly to understand one's scholarly field, in their case Old Testament literature.

This, however, did not mean that Old Testament literature was treated as literature as such, that is, literature to be interpreted for its own sake as any other kind of literature. Old Testament scholarship of the present century has been trying to find what lies *behind* Old Testament literature: profane history, history of religion or history of theology. In the following I shall not produce a *Forschungsgeschichte* of what might be called traditional Old Testament scholarship of the twentieth century. Several fine publications that deal with this issue already exist.[1] On the following pages I shall be tracing some of the tendencies to be found in recent Old Testament historical-critical scholarship that has broken with the traditional approaches, as a background for the presentation of my

---

1. I refer among others to J. Barton, *Reading the Old Testament.* Scandinavian *Forschungsgeschichte* is the subject of K. Jeppesen and B. Otzen (eds.), *The Productions of Time.*

own methodological point of departure for the interpretation of the so-called historical traditions in the book of Hosea. I shall not go into the social or sciento-psychological preconditions of what seems to resemble a scholarly patricide.[2] Indeed, as far as possible I will not join forces with this patricide. But I shall examine the results of it in two fields of research, that are nearest to the 'fathers'.

The first field is the study of the earliest history of Israel, and the second field concerns the criticism that has arisen during the last two decades against the classical Documentary Hypothesis. Certainly, both of these fields employ historical-critical methods. The scholarly rebellion previously mentioned does not reject historical criticism as a valid approach to Old Testament history or history of literature—a tendency applying to other aspects of the 'youth rebellion' that has become more and more established during these years, as for example within American rhetorical criticism or European structuralism. But at the same time it is characteristic for this 'rebellion'—especially for the study of the history of Israel—that the traditional methods of study, which have been mostly based on Old Testament and Near Eastern parallels, are no longer regarded as satisfactory. Modern sociological methods are demanding more and more attention for the scientific study of the history of Israel. As for the study of the literary origin and tradition of the Old Testament—especially with regard to the Pentateuch—by and large scholarship is not departing from well-known methods. But the traditional methods are used with far more scepticism than was the case for previous optimistic scholarship.

The present state of affairs for Old Testament study is marked by a clash between a maximalist and a minimalist approach to the material. The maximalist Old Testament scholar believes that the material is *de facto* telling something about what the text is dealing with at first sight. It is then the task of the scholar to find the historical facts that lie behind the information. This is the case whether one is trying to find the original historical occurrences or the original narrative. Thus, the scholars can be compared to wood carvers, carving their materials, with chips of wood

---

2. An example of this kind of 'patricide' is B.J. Diebner's introduction to H. Friis: *Die Bedingungen für die Errichtung des Davidischen Reichs in Israel und seiner Umwelt*, pp. 217-41. Cf. also H. Friis, 'Ein neues Paradigma für die Erforschung der Vorgeschichte Israels?', originally presented as an introduction to a discussion at the Old Testament Colloquium, University of Copenhagen, 1977.

flying around their ears, until they have found their way to the figures
hiding inside the original wooden block. The onlooker, then, at the conclusion of the work, can applaud, shouting for joy: 'How did you know
that this was inside?'

The maximalist scholar is presupposing that inside the belaboured
textual corpus genuine historical information is hidden, which can tell
about the earliest history and narrative art of Israel. What counts is to
cut away the accretions—they can be scrapped as 'secondary'—and
reach the kernel. A reductionist approach to the material is clearly
prevalent. Scholarship can 'reduce' its way to what in all probability is
the historical kernel. At the same time the maximalist is inspired by
optimism about the size of this kernel. A characteristic phrase is: 'Es
lässt sich nicht beweisen, Tatsache aber ist...'[3] Concerning literary composition the same attitude is maintained. Behind the accretions of the
narratives the original layers can be found by removing redactional
layers, often easily recognizable by their ideological *Tendenz*. When this
tendency has been cut away, one is left with the valuable material, that
is, the original text.

This presentation might be called a caricature. However, it is not my
aim to accuse maximalist scholarship of a lack of seriousness. The point
is to find the reason for the emergence of minimalist scholarship, which
has both deep confidence and deep suspicion of the texts. This combination might seem paradoxical. But if we hope to understand what is going
on during this period we have to accept and understand this paradox.

The minimalist confidence in the texts is—since the search for the
kernel has proven hazardous—first and foremost found in keeping to
the Masoretic Text (MT) and only reluctantly correcting it.[4] The concept
of 'the original author' is not the item of examination. The exegete
focuses attention on the last redactional stage, trying to specify which
message this final redaction has put into the text.[5] Or one goes one step
further as, for example, Brevard S. Childs. In his *Introduction to the Old
Testament as Scripture*, Childs insists on analysing the individual Old
Testament books in their canonical context, in that the formation of the

3. See B.J. Diebner's so-named article with the subtitle: 'Sprachfigur statt
Methode in der kritischen Erforschung des AT'.
4. But see N.P. Lemche, 'Kan man knuse jern, jern fra nord, og bronze',
pp. 61-65.
5. So, for example, Robert P. Carroll and Gale A. Yee (see below).

books was influenced by their authoritative status.[6] The final canonical form of the books provides the critical norm for the exegete.[7] Yet another path is followed by B.J. Diebner, who maintains that an investigation of the reception of the texts (*Rezensions-Kritik*) is *de facto* the only possible one.

Along with this confidence in the texts as they stand we find a deep mistrust in the possibility that they should say anything at all about the time they 'claim' to speak about. If we are looking for information about Israel's so-called pre-national period it is useless to rely on the books of Joshua or Judges: an immigration has never occurred (what these 'sources' want to do is to address Judah in exile or post-exilic Judaism), the narratives in Genesis and Exodus are without *historical* reality, and so forth.

Behind this combination of trust and mistrust is the demand for *verification* and *verifiability*. Whatever cannot be verified is suspicious. This principle is at the same time both sound and dangerous. It prevents, of course, the possibility that a hypothesis forms the point of departure for 'totally safe insights'. But at the same time one runs the risk of putting scholarly fantasy in the doghouse together with curiosity.

Methodological Remarks—Tradition and History

The intention of the present study is to make a traditio-historical examination of the traditions about Israel's past as they appear in the book of Hosea: what is their background, and how does Hosea use them?[8]

With regard to historical veracity, I do not claim that the traditions about Israel's past necessarily imply that there once was an historical Jacob struggling with God, a historical Exodus or historical wanderings of the children of Israel in the Sinai desert. It is impossible to trace the traditions back to their historical origins or narratological sources, that is,

---

6. 'The authoritative Word gave the community its form and content in obedience to the divine imperative, yet conversely the reception of the authoritative tradition by its hearers gave shape to the same writings through a historical and theological process of selecting, collecting, and ordering. The formation of the canon was not a late extrinsic validation of a corpus of writings, but involved a series of decisions deeply affecting the shape of the books.' Childs, *Introduction to the Old Testament as Scripture*, pp. 58-59.

7. Childs, *Introduction*, p. 76.

8. For the problem of the 'Hosea *persona*' and redaction criticism, see below, pp. 15ff.

their 'kernel'. Early Scandinavian scholarship had a very optimistic view of the possibilities that lay in following the paths of tradition, an idea that was based on the assumption of the existence of a long, conservative, oral transmission.[9] But this optimism is now rejected by, for example, N.P. Lemche.[10] Concerning 'historical' value of the sources he claims,

> Indeed, if one retains the notion of a patriarchal age, the distance between the patriarchs and the writing down of the sources is easily at least a thousand years. *The gap between written fixation and the 'underlying events' is too great to permit us to accept the tradition as a primary source for our reconstruction of the past.* [...] The notion of a special 'patriarchal age' has been shown to be a *fata morgana*.[11]

It is, therefore, hazardous to use the texts as sources of the history of pre-national or even premonarchical Israel.[12] And—it should be added—unnecessary in our connection. For the use of the traditions of Israel's past in the book of Hosea is totally independent of their historical veracity. Their theological veracity is of another kind, resting as it does on the tradition's ability to speak of the recipient's relationship with God.

Methodological Remarks—Tradition and Redaction

The Traditional Views
It is commonly supposed that the Hosean traditions were preserved for posterity by refugees from the Northern Kingdom of Israel. After the fall of Samaria in 722 BCE what has been called 'Hosea's literary remains'[13] were taken to Judah and put together, forming our present book of Hosea. Hosea's oracles concerning the fall of Israel had proven to hold true, and his words fell on fertile soil in Judah, because he had also spoken about Judah itself on several occasions. The present composition of the book of Hosea is traceable to a Judaean redaction.[14]

This is—shortly put—the view of the German Old Testament scholar

---

9. See Engnell, *Gamla Testamentet*, pp. 39-44; E. Nielsen, *Oral Tradition*, pp. 18-38.

10. Lemche, *Early Israel*, pp. 377-85, especially pp. 380-81.

11. Lemche, *Early Israel*, pp. 377-78, Lemche's italics.

12. See further Lemche, *Early Israel*, p. 379. The same conviction is prevalent in *Toward a Consensus on the Emergence of Israel in Canaan* (ed. D. Edelman).

13. W. Rudolph, *Hosea*, p. 25.

14. Rudolph, *Hosea*, p. 25.

Wilhelm Rudolph. Neither he nor his compatriot Hans Walther Wolff supposes that the book of Hosea has undergone thorough—that is, essentially modifying—theological reworkings. As to composition Wolff claims that the book of Hosea consists of three parts, chs. 1–3, 4–11 and 12–14.[15] Parts of the written tradition—mainly in the first part of the book—stem from the prophet himself. But the main part of the Hosean tradition, that is, parts II and III, is due to contemporary sketches, the so-called *Auftrittsskizzen*. Hosea's preaching to his listeners is here delineated, and it is their reactions, that is, their acclamations or contradictions, that can be heard between the individual kerygmatic units. They are put into writing by '[Hosea's] circles (...) who were devoted to him from the outset and supported him during perilous times'.[16]

The three main parts of the book of Hosea embody the same structure, in that they all begin with doom and conclude with vows of redemption. They have been composed in different ways and by different redactors, but these redactors all belong to the party that was loyal to Yahweh, and of which party Hosea is considered to be a prominent member. Wolff believes that the members of this party were the predecessors of the Deuteronomic movement. The ideas of this movement can be traced through the entire book, from the prophet's own lifetime down until the time of the Babylonian exile.

In addition, two Judaean redactions—an earlier and a later—can be found. Supposedly, the final collection of the three parts has taken place at the same time as the final redaction, that is, when 1.1 and 14.10 were added.

The Critique of the Traditional View

As shown above, twentieth-century research on Hosea until c. 1975 can be described as maximalist. The book of Hosea is considered to be a valid source for reconstructing the life and theology of the prophet Hosea himself. But since 1975 the minimalist position has been addressing the questions mentioned above to the book of Hosea as well as to other prophetic books: is it possible to maintain confidence in the book as a source for determining the life and theology of a prophet? Is it possible

---

15. So Wolff, in his introduction to the composition of the book of Hosea in *Hosea*, pp. xxix-xxxii. Differently, for example, Rudolph, *Hosea*.

16. 'Kreise [...], die Hosea von Anfang an zugetan waren und die auch in den Tagen der Bedrohung zu ihm hielten' (Wolff, *Hosea*, pp. xxx).

to get back to the prophet's *ipsissima verba*? And is there any reason to do so?

Accordingly, the book of Hosea as well as other prophetic books are studied with regard to the question of the *cui bono* of the redaction. The final redaction has thereby become the main object of inquiry. The scope has now been extended beyond the questions posed in earlier times, which aimed at separating authentic sayings from secondary, and which, it is said, regarded the 'authentic' or 'original' sayings as being more valuable than the 'secondary'.[17] There has also been special interest in the possibility of an exilic influence on the prophetic books. For example, a Deuteronomistic redaction of the book of Amos was demonstrated by Werner H. Schmidt as early as 1965.[18] With regard to the book of Isaiah an examination of the relationship between Proto- and Deutero-Isaiah has led some scholars, for example Knud Jeppesen, to the conclusion that Deutero-Isaiah was the redactor of Proto-Isaiah.[19] Jeppesen argues that a similar exilic redaction of the book of Micah took place.[20] Minimalist principles have been employed with extreme sharpness by Robert P. Carroll, in his examinations of the book of Jeremiah,[21] and by Gale A. Yee in her study of the book of Hosea.

17. The book of Isaiah is separated into the 'authentic' Isaiah-material from the eighth-century and Deutero-Isaiah (and possibly Trito-Isaiah) from exilic (and post-exilic) times. Another example is Mowinckel's division of the book of Jeremiah into four sources. Cf. also Duhm's somewhat different division based on metrical considerations. Incidentally, Duhm is one of the most outstanding examples of a scholar who separates what is 'authentic' from what is 'secondary'; see, for example, his famous commentary from 1901, *Das Buch Jeremia*, xvi-xxii.

18. W.H. Schmidt, 'Die deuteronomistische Redaktion des Amosbuches. Zu den theologischen Unterschieden zwischen dem Prophetenwort und seinem Sammler', pp. 188-93.

19. K. Jeppesen, *Græder ikke*, pp. 73-80. This assumption does not, however, reign supreme. See, for example, M.A. Sweeney, who in his PhD thesis, 'Isaiah 1–4 and the Post-Exilic Understanding of the Isaianic Tradition', draws the conclusion that 'the editors of the book [i.e. the book of Isaiah] fashioned chapters 1–39 as a preface for chapters 40–66. This means that the early Isaianic tradition found in chapters 1–39, was interpreted, supplemented, edited, and presented in relation to Deutero-Isaiah and Trito-Isaiah. In essence the concerns of *the latter part* of the book dictated the final redaction of the first part' (p. 185, my italics); cf. also R. Rendtorff, 'Zur Komposition des Buches Jesaja'.

20. The redaction of Micah is the subject of Jeppesen, *Græder ikke*.

21. R.P. Carroll, *Jeremiah* (Carroll is building mainly on the works of E.W. Nicholson and W. Thiel); G.A. Yee, *Composition*.

Yee's thesis is an intensive, radical study of the redaction and composition of the book of Hosea. Indeed, it seems at first sight most 'secure'
to follow the way Yee works back from the book's final redacted stage
to the earlier stages. Her methods need modification, however. I shall
return to Yee's study in the following paragraph, after offering an
account of my own view.

Methodological Considerations

If modern Pentateuchal criticism is right[22]—and it will be the methodological precondition of what follows that it is—then the book of Hosea
presents *the earliest written fixation of the traditions of Jacob and of*

22. By modern Pentateuchal criticism is meant those investigations of the
Pentateuch that during the last 20–25 years have made a critique of the classical
Documentary Hypothesis. As typical examples of modern Pentateuchal critics Rolf
Rendtorff and H.H. Schmid are often mentioned. Both of them published mono-
graphs in the mid-seventies on Pentateuchal problems (Rendtorff, *Das überlieferungsgeschichtliche Problem des Pentateuch*, Schmid, *Der sogenannte Jahwist*). However,
both of them seem—as almost exclusively German language oriented scholars—to be
totally uninfluenced by the some 30 years older so-called Scandinavian school.
Especially Ivan Engnell in his *Gamla Testamentet*, I, rebelled against both textual and
literary criticism as well as against the commonly accepted dating of the sources of
the Tetrateuch. Engnell rejects talking about sources, being of the opinion that a long
oral tradition has been in existence, transmitted by different circles of narrators
(*Gamla Testamentet*, I, p. 214 *et passim*). The Scandinavian version of Tradition
History never came to the fore in the German-speaking world, partly due to the
religio-historical trend specific to the Scandinavian school (and to Anglo-Saxon
Patternism or the Myth-and-Ritual School). German *Überlieferungsgeschichte* with
its basis in the Documentary Hypothesis attained its full scope in Claus Westermann's impressive commentary on Genesis (BKAT I/1-3). Westermann's commentary can be viewed as the ultimate culmination of a scholarly method, which since the
time of the publication of the commentary should not remain unquestioned.
   One aspect of modern Pentateuchal criticism is a new departure with regard to the
literary genesis of *Exodus–Numbers*. Schmid has been posing questions to the
existence of a continuous source, J, outside Genesis, and Martin Rose's publications
have demonstrated a close connection between the Yahwist and the Deuteronomist.
For the present investigations the most relevant result of recent research is the late
dating of the traditions of the patriarchs and of the wandering in the wilderness, which
was argued first and foremost in Rendtorff's and Schmid's publications in Germany
and the almost contemporary publications by John Van Seters and T.L. Thompson in
America. On this complex of problems, see *JSOT* 2.3 (1977), which was dedicated to
the issue of Pentateuchal criticism, and Lemche, *Early Israel*, pp. 357-85.

Israel's past. This claim may seem both uncritical, old-fashioned and naive against the background of the views mentioned above. Indeed, modern scholarship has made a good case for minimalist redaction criticism and its insights seem in many cases to be convincing. Nevertheless, it is the view of the present study that Wolff's opinion concerning the redaction of the book of Hosea is by and large to be followed. This does not mean that we should *a priori* regard the information given in the introduction of a certain prophetic book as 'the truth, the whole truth, and nothing but the truth'. Questions like those posed by R.P. Carroll remain valid: How can we know if the prophet Hosea (if such a person ever existed) or others are responsible for the individual oracles?

We cannot, of course. No one has found a scroll with Hosea's own handwriting on it, scientifically datable by the means of the carbon-14 dating method to the year 723 BC. Yet, there would appear to be reasons for not rejecting out of hand the possibility that behind the traditions transmitted there was in fact a historical person, the prophet Hosea. One could ask: if it is possible to establish the existence of a certain consistency in terminology, motive and theology in a particular prophetic book, is it not possible, then, to argue for the probability of what could be called 'the consistency of the author'?[23]

If there is any vestige of truth in what we claim to know about the actions of the Old Testament prophets as oral preachers, then there has at least been transmitted a rendering—admittedly not precisely datable—of what was found important by the tradents. We posses the words of the prophet, but in a redacted, and that means an elaborated, form. That means, in addition, that we must recognize the possibility that the prophet has proclaimed a greater number of oracles than those that have been transmitted, including oracles that are different from those transmitted.[24] Accordingly, our picture of what is 'genuine' remains at best incomplete, at worst distorted.

The dating of Old Testament texts—or at least of their present and redacted form—to the time of the exile, is a major trend in modern Old Testament scholarship. In fact a late dating of the Pentateuch as well as of the Deuteronomistic History and of the prophetic books is most convincing. The traces of exilic problems that present themselves when reading, for example, an Old Testament prophetic book, should not be

23. And is it possible for us to do better than to 'render probable'—will it ever be possible to 'prove'?
24. Cf. further for this complex of problems K. Jeppesen, *Græder ikke*, pp. 100ff.

ignored. The presence of these kinds of traces will, accordingly, be evidence that it is not always in a certain prophetic book the prophet, whose name is mentioned in the preamble, who is speaking.

Yet, conversely, if a text in no ways exhibits traces of a later time and its thought, then we can date it to the time from which the text itself claims to stem.[25] Precisely the presence of visible traces of later elaboration of certain texts necessitates, correspondingly, that we must allow for the possibility that other texts—or parts of texts—may stem from the ostensible author when such traces are absent. So, when Martti Nissinen poses the question, 'Does the burden of proof in fact always rest on those who would deny the authenticity of this or that passage?'[26] the answer will be: 'Yes, it does'. It should be added, however, that it is only on rare occasions that traces of redaction are totally absent. And the interest of the exilic period in guilt, punishment and the possibility of a return from Babylon is prominent among these traces.

Certainly, it is the legitimate concern of historical-critical scholarship to seek the traces of the interests of periods later than that of the 'primary author'. But when seeking these traces, we are obliged to be very careful in choosing our criteria of 'primary' and 'secondary' and of how the results obtained are used. We are persistently at risk of falling into that hermeneutical ditch into which the earlier *literar-kritische* scholars have been accused of throwing themselves.

It must at the outset be allowed for that the text has made sense prior to the form presently known. And we must allow for the possibility that 'the author' had various points of view. Is it, for example, totally impossible that a prophet could preach both doom and deliverance? *Aporiae* cannot be used as a criterion for the isolation of later redactional strata without further ado.

I shall elucidate this methodological point of view by contrasting it to Gale A. Yee's. Her PhD-thesis from 1985, 'Composition and Tradition

---

25. So is, too, the point of view of Erling Hammershaimb in his article 'Some Leading Ideas in the Book of Micah': 'in general my guiding rule will be to accept the tradition for those parts of the book where no compelling reasons can be urged against their authenticity, and I shall assume that the ideas appearing in them are an expression of the views of the prophet Micah himself' (E. Hammershaimb, *Some Aspects of Old Testament Prophecy from Isaiah to Malachi*, p. 29).

26. '...ob die Beweislast wirklich immer denjenigen aufgebürdet werden kann, die die Hoseanität dieses oder jenes Stückes bestreiten wollen' (M. Nissinen, *Prophetie, Redaktion und Fortschreibung im Hoseabuch*, p. 39).

in the Book of Hosea: A Redaction Critical Investigation', is an example *inter omnia* of a minimalist method. Yee severely criticizes tradition theories of the composition of Hosea. Her claim is that scholarship has been skewed by presuppositions of the above mentioned kind which she lists as follows:

    I.   The 'original' is the most valuable.

    II. The oral or preliterary stage is the proper focus of research for understanding the prophetic message.

    III. There is no qualitative difference between the oral and written stages.[27]

Against these methodological pitfalls Yee argues for '...a redaction critical investigation which *begins* with the final redacted state of the text and *then* proceeds to discuss its earlier stages of tradition'.[28]

Yee chooses to view the book of Hosea as the work of one single author, namely 'the final redactor who used literary traditions attributed to Hosea'.[29] When she so to speak has come to know this author and the structure that he has imposed on the book, and when she has identified the religio-political thrust of the selection and composition of the material, then she believes herself to have 'a more secure foundation to deal with the question of older traditions in the text'.[30]

Yee uses two main criteria in her redaction-critical endeavour, the first of which is the presence of aporiae, the second an analysis of the structure of the final redaction. When it comes to structure Yee sees Hosea 1–3 as giving clues to the internal thrust of the final redaction. She argues for the existence of four stages in the composition of the book of Hosea.[31]

---

27. These presuppositions are the subject of Yee's chapter 2, cited from the titles of the paragraphs of the chapter, *Composition*, pp. 27-50.

28. Yee, *Composition*, xi, Yee's italics.

29. Yee, *Composition*, p. 48.

30. Yee, *Composition*, pp. 48-49.

31. Since the final form for Yee 'embodies a gestaltist unity from the different phases of the tradition', Yee avoids 'vocabulary like "strata, layers, and accretions" that highlights the disunity or disconnectedness of the text rather than its unity. The different stages build upon each other and exist in a relational function with each other' (Yee, *Composition*, p. 305). The list of the stages is based on Yee's concluding ch. 8 (*Composition*, pp. 305-13).

I.   *Hosea—H*, traditions stemming from the prophet Hosea himself.
II.   *The Collector—C*, who created the first 'written tradition of the Hosean sayings'. A few traditions in Hosea 1 and 2 are composed by C.
III.   *The First Redactor—R1*, a Judaean with a certain likeness to the redactor who wrote the first edition of The Deuteronomistic History at the time of Josiah, and
IV.   *The Final Redactor—R2*. Working at the time of the exile, the final redactor is responsible for the present book of Hosea, its contents and its structure. R2 provides the book with the redactional beginning, Hos. 1.1. In addition, he inserts the three *Heilsgeschichtlich* chapters, 3, 11 and 14, thus creating the three-part structure of the book, and he adds the concluding remark, Hos. 14.10. Moreover, the work of R2 is interwoven into that of R1.

As previously mentioned, Yee wants to secure her methodological objectivity by working her way backwards from the final stage to the prior strata. But her method would appear to be resemble the common, old-fashioned *Literar-Kritik*, from which she wants so deeply to separate herself, using *aporiae* as a criterion for an isolation of redactional strata in a certain text. Accordingly, Yee is not from the outset allowing for the possibility of an extended, varied theology in the first strata of the text. With her redaction-critical dissecting knife she divides the book of Hosea into layers, each with a separate interest and intention. This attitude is— by the way—a mark of many others who share Yee's scholarly interests.[32]

Yee is also in another fashion following a modern trend. Without specifically mentioning it, she belongs to a scholarly school that believes that the main *Sitz-im-Leben* of almost all Old Testament literature is to be found during the period of the Babylonian Exile. And that seems to be the primary reason why she wants to see Israel's return from the exile as the main incentive for the composition of the book of Hosea. With this as her point of departure she is proposing an exilic intention for the final redaction, which at first—and second—glance can be hard to recognize.[33]

32. As an example can be mentioned Ina Willi-Plein, *Vorformen der Schriftexegese innerhalb des Alten Testaments*.

33. Yee finds the exilic interest in Hos. 12, for example, but see below, pp. 49-51.

Yet, there might be another explanation for those traces of the exile which can be identified in the book of Hosea. It should be recognized that the book of Hosea in all probability underwent its own *Judaean* exile. If it is at all possible to speak of a source for the redacted prophetic book—and in my opinion anything else is questionable[34]—then this source presumably was brought to Judah after the fall of Samaria by a circle of Hosea's disciples,[35] as commonly claimed by Old Testament scholarship. In spite of the biblical presentation of Israel and Judah as sister-nations, the feelings between the two were, in fact, not always totally tender. So, some of what Yee sees as indisputably exilic may well express influence of this Judaean exile.

As to the question of redaction, it has been claimed that redactors can work by other means than accretions and glosses. In his monograph on Micah, *Græder ikke saa saare*, K. Jeppesen introduces the metaphor of the redactional *patchwork*.[36] A patchwork is a carpet, made up of older

34. This can be seen, for example, from the Hosean influence on the book of Jeremiah (see below Chapter 5).

35. On the beginnings of a prophetic tradition, Jeppesen (following among others D.R. Jones) urges that 'The beginning of the formation of the tradition occurred when the prophet gave his 'sealed' message to his disciples with what amounts to an act of ordination. [...] it is doubtful whether a long tradition process can be imagined unless there from the very beginning had been stories, *legends*, about the prophet to which the oracles could be connected' (*Græder ikke*, p. 96). This statement can be seen as a corrective to Carroll's aforementioned skepticism about the reality of the 'genuine' prophet—or at least of the possibility and sense of finding the 'genuine' prophet (Carroll, *Jeremiah, passim*).

36. 'A patchwork rug is produced by using patches from different pieces of clothing; if it is home-made, it is normally made of materials that come from the articles of clothing of one and the same family. But one patch comes from a pair of trousers, another from a blouse, and in between one can perhaps find the remains of patchwork from a rug that has already been worn out. The only changes that have taken place are perhaps that the edges have been trimmed. Regardless of what the original materials were used for, one will—providing one is sufficiently dexterous— finally get what one wants, a sleeping rug, for example. [...] prophetic books can *mutatis mutandis* be compared with such a home-made patchwork rug made by people who had a need for a message that could explain and encourage. On the one hand, they wished to maintain that they made use of a particular earlier prophet's words in order to make sense of their own time. On the other hand, it was decisive that the prophecies fit the situation. Therefore, they took as needed from the existing legends and collections of oracles that were connected to the prophet's name—they took words and sentences and even whole sections, and they joined them together to create a new whole' (Jeppesen, *Græder ikke*, p. 125).

patches. For our purposes, this means that a prophetic book can be viewed as having been put together by the redactors, who used oracles and traditions that were related to the named prophet. Oracles, *per se*, can thus be seen as consisting of patches 'sown' together during an earlier period. Accordingly several redactional layers can exist side by side. But in the final redactional stage these oracles and traditions are structured in such a way that they speak to the issues of the moment.

Jeppesen uses the patchwork metaphor in his search for the theological influence of the exilic period on the book of Micah. But the possibility exists that this method was used by redactors prior to the exile. This point will be demonstrated in the exegesis of Hosea 12 (Chapter 2, below). However, the patchwork theory does not allow for a total rediscovery of the *ipsissima vox prophetae*. It is not possible—or necessary—to distinguish between the prophet and the tradition about him. But it is possible to uncover the first collections of the Hosean traditions.

On the other hand, it is, of course, not the claim of the present work that everything in the book of Hosea indiscriminately stems from the first tradents of Hosean theology. Certain possibilities exist for discriminating between 'Hosean' material and accretions, the best examples being the Judaean glosses or 'emendations'. It is only possible in a very few instances to demonstrate 'totally safe' traces of early redactional glosses—and conversely, only on rare instances, if any, is it possible to recognize the *ipsissima vox Hoseae*. What we have access to is a theology belonging in a certain geographical and religious milieu, a certain time and usage of language.

Thus, as indicated above (p. 19), no better explanation has been proposed for the transmission of the material now collected in the book of Hosea than that of H.W. Wolff, that is, that a circle of Hosean disciples, fleeing to Judah after the fall of Samaria, collected and wrote down what they remembered of the words of the prophet Hosea.

So, 'Hosea says', means: 'The eldest tradition available of the prophet Hosea says'. Taking this as our point of departure, it makes sense to look behind the final redaction of the book of Hosea for the earliest written form of the traditions of Israel's past—in other words, to go about the task not only with the help of redaction criticism but also with the methods of tradition history. Whether Hosea is discontinuous with the tradition, as urged by J. Vollmer,[37] or rearranges and develops it,[38] he in any case is dependent on the previous tradition that must have been known by his audience.[39] The traditions in the book of Hosea can be viewed as mere myth or myth in the disguise of 'history'.[40] It is not necessary to make a sharp distinction. They function as a sort of 'Creation-mythology' of the Land of Israel and of its relationship to Yahweh. Hosea is not interested in mere history-telling but in its effect on his contemporaries.[41]

Accordingly, as pointed out before, it is not the significance of the book of Hosea for history that is the scope of the present thesis. The exegetical study of the book of Hosea is necessitated by its significance for understanding the theology of the book of Hosea itself, and for the history of Israelite religion and Old Testament theology.

The Composition of the Book of Hosea
As I have mentioned, H.W. Wolff, followed by many others (for example Gale A. Yee), divides the book of Hosea into three parts: Hosea 1–3, 4–11 and 12–14. Each of these parts consists of oracles of doom, followed by oracles of salvation. Wolff's description is by and large followed here. The caesura between Hosea 3 and 4 is evident, the gulf between Hosea 11 and 12 less so.

The work of the exilic or post-exilic redactor is evident in the preamble, Hos. 1.1, which dates the prophet's office in the same way as the preambles of other prophetic books within or outside the book of the 12 Minor Prophets.[42] The closing remarks, Hos. 14.10, also belong to this

37. Vollmer, *Geschichtliche Rückblicke*, p. 124.
38. R. Kümpel, *Berufung Israels*, p. 193.
39. That Hosea uses traditions known to his audience can be seen from the way he 'tells his tales' in Hos. 12, for example. Cf. below, Chapter 2.
40. I use the term 'Myth' in a broader sense than it is used by Gunkel and the scholarly tradition that takes its point of departure in his work. Cf. H.J.L. Jensen, 'Den strukturelle myteanalyse–og Det gamle Testamente'; *idem*, 'Mytebegrebet i den historisk-kritiske og i den strukturalistiske forskning'.
41. Cf. K.W. Whitelam, 'Between History and Literature: The Social Production of Israel's Traditions of Origin', pp. 66ff.
42. The superscription consists perhaps of two layers: 1. an earlier superscription, תחלת דבר־יהוה בהושע, followed by the formula ויאמר יהוה אל־הושע, which introduced the material that was handed over to the final redactor; 2. the final redaction, dating Hosea in relation to the Judaean kings, probably as a part of the mutual redaction of the prophetic books presumably in the exilic or post-exilic era. Cf. also Yee, *Composition*, pp. 55-57.

late redactional stratum. These two verses form the cognitive framework, which has been given to the complete book of Hosea by the final redactor.

Thematizations are found, too, in the discrete parts of the book: The first part (Hos. 1–3) is organized around the theme of 'Hosea's Marriage'. Here we find the linking of prophetic legend and prophetic words, which Jeppesen holds to be the first stratum in the history of a given prophetic tradition.[43] The three chapters form a collection centred around the preaching of Hosea 2.[44] With the exception of Hos. 1.1 we find only two instances of late exilic interest, namely the promise of a multitude and the commentary on the names of the prophet's children, Hos. 2.1-3, and the promise of return, Hos. 3.5.[45]

The second part of the book of Hosea has an analogous preamble, Hos. 4.1-3.[46] It functions as the superscription for a collection of Hosean oracles that describe the religious and political apostasy in Israel up until 722 BCE. The various parts are collected in kerygmatic units that do not seem to follow an intelligible plan of any kind. On the other hand, a thematizing tendency can be traced—the separate units are not collected in a totally haphazard fashion. E.M. Good sees the second part of the book of Hosea as consisting of thematic collections of smaller kerygmatic units, as for example Hos. 9.10–11.11; 12. In addition, precisely because of the thematic agreement between Hos. 9.10–11.11 and Hosea 12–13, it is worth considering if it is reasonable to regard Hosea 12–14 as a self-contained third part of the book of Hosea, like Wolff and others do, or whether Hosea 4–14 should rather be regarded as one unit.

Accordingly, the second unit is framed by exilic super- and postscripts, leading the unit from the theme of doom to a promise of salvation. The single parts of the second unit stem from the Hosean tradition, while the redaction and composition have been undertaken by the redactor who

---

43. Jeppesen, *Græder ikke*, pp. 96ff.
44. Cf. further E.M. Good, 'The Composition of Hosea', pp. 27-30.
45. Cf. the exilic text Jer. 3.18. Hos. 2.23-25 may be viewed the same way. Hos. 3, the second legend of Hosea's marriage, written in the first person, is seen by Yee as the exilic closing of the marriage narrative, built on the simile narrative of Hos. 1. This does not seem to be a necessary conclusion. Only Hos. 3.5 bears marks of later accretions; cf. Good, 'The Composition of Hosea'; Wolff, *Hosea*, p. 57; Clements, *Prophecy and Tradition*, p. 30. Differently, G.I. Emmerson, *Hosea*, pp. 101-105, 113.
46. Cf. J. Jeremias, 'Hosea 4–7. Beobachtungen zur Komposition des Buches Hosea', p. 49; Good, 'The Composition of Hosea', p. 30.

addressed Judah with the message that if they did not learn from the destiny of Israel and trust in their mutual God, Yahweh Sebaoth, they would experience the same fate as Israel's. But if they listened and amended their ways, the promises would be for them, as well.

Using the patchwork metaphor, the book of Hosea is sewn together of two rugs, each consisting of smaller units, collected by a group of refugees from Israel, arriving at Judah after the fall of Samaria. The collection of the two patchwork rugs took place (presumably) in Jerusalem, before the fall of the city in 587 BCE. The marriage narrative was placed before the more concrete attacks on a wayward cult as a key to understanding. Its message consisted of doom and hope as well: Yahweh wanted to purify his apostate love of his youth, the Chosen People, so that it could 'blossom like the vine, their fragrance [...] be like the wine of Lebanon' (Hos. 14.8 [MT]).[47]

47. Another view is posed by M. Nissinen, *Prophetie, Redaktion und Fortschreibung im Hoseabuch*. Following the idea of a so-called 'Rolling corpus', first posed by W. McKane in connection with the book of Jeremiah, and using the techniques of colometry, he concludes that 'the concepts of redaction and updating partially intersect. Every redactional measure is at the same time an updating of the text in question...Furthermore, several pieces of updated material may have been composed by the same hand...without there necessarily being a question of an all-embracing and well planned redaction. The material in the book of Hosea thus cannot be completely attributed to a few single redactions. A considerable portion of the text apparently goes back to a sporadic updating made by countless authors (*Hände*), which was hardly planned but rather inspired by certain portions of the text...the entire text, as found at that time, served as a draft (*Vorlage*) for the contemporaneous redaction and updating...' (pp. 341-42).

Part I

EXEGESIS

Chapter 2

HOSEA'S JACOB

In this chapter we shall examine the traditions about the Northern Kingdom's special patriarch, Jacob, that are found in Hosea 12. Is Jacob a hero or a villain? How does the book of Hosea use its traditional material? These questions are to be answered within the framework of redaction criticism, and we must, therefore, first turn our attention to the chapter's structure.

The Structure of Hosea 12

The structure of Hosea 12 is as follows:

vv. 1-2	Ephraim and Judah are faithless
vv. 3-7	The Jacob traditions
vv. 8-9	Canaan and Ephraim are faithless
vv. 10-11	The Exodus will be repeated
v. 12	The worship of idols in Gilead and Gilgal
vv. 13-14	The Jacob tradition and the Exodus tradition
v. 15	The bloodguilt of Ephraim must be punished.[1]

We can observe at the outset a shift between the statements about Ephraim concerning the present situation and the traditions from Israel's past. In 12.12 the name Ephraim is, to be sure, not mentioned, but Gilead and Gilgal are within Israelite territory, and this fact gives the statement relevance for the present.

Scholars have suggested a number of different rearrangements of the

---

1. Hos. 13.1-3 is regarded by some commentators as a continuation of 12.15. The fact that Hos. 12–14 constitutes a larger unit, however, speaks against the necessity of a close connection between 13.1-3 and 12.15. The relationship between 13.1-3 and 12.15 can be explained on the basis of the larger context, and 12.15 is best regarded as the conclusion to the *rîb*, which has its beginning in 12.3.

pericopes in the Hosea 12.[2] None of the suggested 'improvements' is convincing when the structure of the chapter is taken into consideration along with the unified character of 12.3-7, to which we shall return below. It is quite striking that all of the statements in the chapter that deal with the present situation are condemnatory. How does it stand with those statements that deal with the past?

Jacob and Israel, Hosea 12.3-7

v. 3   The Lord has an indictment against Israel,[3]
and will punish Jacob according to his ways,
and repay him according to his deeds.

v. 4   In the womb he supplanted his brother,
and in his manhood he strove with God.

v. 5   He strove with the angel and prevailed,
he wept and sought his favor;
he met him at Bethel,
and there he spoke with him.

v. 6   Yahweh the God of hosts,
Yahweh is his name.

v. 7   With your God's help, you shall return.
Hold fast to love and justice
put always hope in your God.[4]

2.   Rudolph reads vv. 13-14 after v. 10 (*Hosea*, pp. 220-25), while Ginsberg makes a radical rearrangement of the chapter and reads vv. 13-14 after v. 6 and understands v. 7 as the conclusion of the chapter ('Hosea's Ephraim, More Fool Than Knave: A New Interpretation of Hosea 12.1-14', pp. 341-42). In this regard, Good rightly notes: 'It would be interesting to hear his (i.e. Ginsberg's) explanation of the process through which the oracle became so stupidly disarranged as he suggests' ('Hosea and the Jacob Tradition', p. 148 n. 2).

3.   MT reads Judah, but the text is often corrected to read Israel (with *BHSb*). The fact that the word-pair Judah/Jacob is not entirely unknown supports MT (see Jeppesen, *Græder ikke*, pp. 146 and 148). It is also unnecessary to regard all of the Judah passages in the book of Hosea as later redactional insertions (see Emmerson, *Hosea, passim*). On the other hand, it would seem rather obvious to regard the Judah reading here as a later insertion. The identification Jacob/Israel is indeed fundamental for an understanding of the pericope, and the correction is further supported by the word plays יעקב/עקב and ישראל/שרה. The correction of ישראל to יהודה is best understood as redactional (see in this regard Ginsberg, 'Hosea's Ephraim', p. 342; Good, 'Hosea and the Jacob Tradition', p. 139; Emmerson, *Hosea*, p. 63 and below).

4.   Verses 4 and 7 are translated by me; v. 7 is translated in accordance with the Authorized Danish Version which is closer to MT. Differently NRSV.

Hosea 12.3-7 can be form-critically classified as a so-called *rîb*-statement, within which it is stated that Yahweh has an indictment against Israel and will punish Jacob. Verses 3 and 7 provide a framework for the interpretation of the Jacob traditions, but the function of v. 6 can first be determined after a closer analysis. Correspondingly, it is first necessary to investigate the Jacob pericope itself before making an investigation of the entire pericope in order to determine which traditions are being referred to. It will then be possible to ask the question as to how the Jacob material is being employed theologically as well as who is using this material.

The exegetical literature on Hosea 12 abounds with attempts to identify the events that are spoken of in vv. 4-5. The fact that there is only limited agreement between the Jacob traditions of Genesis and those that Hosea refers to has created a number of problems for research. These problems have, meanwhile, a close connection with the view that the Yahwist strand is quite ancient, a view that prevailed until a few years ago. If the traditions concerning Jacob were available in written form at the time of Solomon, then Hosea would have been able to make use of them. If this were the case, then the modern exegete would be able to recreate an agreement with the use of various (artificial!) manoeuvres or, in contrary fashion, would be able to derive theological conclusions from the lack of agreement.

Meanwhile, if the presupposition is that the Jacob traditions were *not* available in written form in the eighth century, then there is no reason to embark upon an investigation of a *literary* connection, chapter for chapter, verse for verse, between the book of Hosea and Genesis. On the other hand, we can first attempt to identify the traditions that lie behind the book of Hosea and Genesis and then inquire as to whether or not they are the same.[5]

---

5.   In recent years the Jacob section in the book of Hosea has been regarded as a clear example of so-called 'inner biblical exegesis', that is to say, that Hosea employed a text that was already in written form as the point of departure for his own sermon. See, for example, L.M. Eslinger, 'Hosea 12.5a and Genesis 32.29: A Study in Inner Biblical Exegesis'; W.C. Kaiser, Jr, 'Inner Biblical Exegesis as a Model for Bridging the "Then" and "Now" Gap: Hosea 12.1-6'. Another variation of this interest is to be found in I. Willi-Plein, *Vorformen der Schriftexegese innerhalb des Alten Testaments*. It is obvious that with the premises that have been set forth in the introduction it will not be possible to deal with these and corresponding points of view.

Verses 4-5a contain four statements about the life of Jacob:

v. 4a	Jacob supplanted his brother in the womb
v. 4b	As an adult he struggled with God (אלהים)
v. 5a	He fought with an angel and won
v. 5a	He wept and sought his favor

These four statements point forward to v. 5b, the Bethel tradition, which connects the Jacob traditions with the present-day situation of the audience.

Hosea 12.4a

בבפן עקב את-אחיו

In the womb he supplanted his brother

The etymology of the name in Hos. 12.4a presumably plays upon the same etymological traditions surrounding the name of Jacob that are found in Gen. 25.21-34; 27.35-36. As Good claims, it could have been Hosea's intention to make allusions to the entire Jacob–Esau conflict without wishing to develop it; but the book of Hosea refers only quite briefly to the עקב traditions without providing them with any narrative development. The aspect of the womb in Genesis 25 is connected with the use of the root עקב as a verb just as in Genesis 27, but the verb is used differently in the two pericopes. Gen. 25.26 transmits the tradition of Jacob holding the heel of his brother while Gen. 27.36 relates the tradition of Jacob supplanting, or even deceiving, his brother. Hos. 12.4a can be regarded as a passage in which the two traditions have been elliptically worked together.[6] In the elliptical version of Hos. 12.4a, therefore, the figure of Jacob does not appear unequivocally as a deceiver, but rather as a figure in whom two possibilities are found: he can appear as a warning and as an example.[7] As we shall see, the same

---

6. As P.R. Ackroyd writes ('Hosea and Jacob', p. 249), it is not easy to determine the precise meaning of the words that are formed on the basis of the root עקב. De Boer suggested in 1946 ('Genesis XXXII$_{23-33}$. Some Remarks on Composition and Character of the Story', p. 161), that Hos. 12.4a should be translated, 'he had hold on the heel of his brother', which translation is found already in KJV and is followed by RSV. This translation is not as unambiguously negative as 'deceived', which is used for example in the Authorized Danish Translation (*bedrog*).

7. The English word 'supplant' captures these two possible meanings. Cf. *Webster's Ninth New Collegiate Dictionary, s.v.* supplant: to overthrow by tripping up, fr. *sub-* + *planta* sole of the foot...1: to supersede (another) esp. by force of treachery 2a (1) *obs: UPROOT* (2): to eradicate and supply a substitute for...b: to

situation obtains in the following passages in the Jacob pericope.

If the reference to the Jacob traditions was not to be completely meaningless for the audience (we must assume that it was not), then we must conclude that these were known.[8] These must have been longer and more developed oral (or written) traditions, to which it was sufficient for the author to allude. The Hosea (-tradent) has not wished to preserve the narratives or to tell them for the first time, which may well have been the case in Genesis. He uses Jacob as an example that does not require a narrative elaboration. On the contrary, he has reduced the traditions, which were already in circulation, to an absolute minimum.

Hosea 12.4b-5a

> ובאונו שרה את־אלהים
> וישר אל־מלאך ויכל בכה ויתחנן־לו

> and in his manhood he strove with God.
> He strove with the angel and prevailed,
> he wept and sought his favor

In Hos. 12.4b-5a the Jacob traditions are continued. The pericope is normally interpreted with the Penuel narrative (Gen. 32.23-33) as its point of departure. Again, we can see how the traditions are used in different ways. There is, however, corresponding to what we observed above, one common feature, namely, the etymology of the name: ישראל/שרה.[9] This pun appears most clearly in Genesis, where it is told why Jacob received this name. Hosea, on the other hand, simply alludes again to a report that must have been known by the audience, but this time to a report of Jacob's struggle. This is why Hosea is able to make his exposition in such abbreviated fashion.

This conciseness creates, on the other hand, certain problems for the present-day reader, since the text leaves the reader with a number of unanswered questions. These are questions that we also suspect lie behind the story as it is told in Genesis, but there an attempt is made to resolve the questions: the story in Genesis does not indicate with whom Jacob struggles (the indefinite איש is used), or why there is a struggle.

take the place of and serve as a substitute for esp. by reason of superior excellence or power, pp. 1185-86.

8.   Thus also de Boer, 'Genesis XXXII$_{23\text{-}33}$', p. 162.

9.   The vocalization of the verb שרה (v. 5a) has occasioned suggestions to make a correction to שרר or שור, but the word-play is thereby destroyed.

What we have in the Genesis account is an inexplicable assault by night, as though made by a thief, who is unwilling to reveal his identity. And even though the assaulter indirectly discloses that he is God in Gen. 32.29, he does not say which god he is: it is up to Jacob (and the listener) to resolve that issue (Gen. 32.30).

Can this lack of clarity in the exposition be accounted for by the existence of two traditions about Jacob's struggle? The structure of Hos. 12.4-5 could possibly support such an hypothesis, since Hos. 12.4-5a can be regarded as having been constructed of 2 × 2 coherent units. Yet, in v. 4 the coherence is established by the use of the words באונו/בבטן, while in v. 5a it would appear that the course of events described constitutes a unit in which there is a progression. It is, therefore, not necessary to read 4b and 5a as parallel units. On the contrary, the structure of the verses would seem to contradict such a reading. Thus, it is possible that there are really two different struggles involving Jacob: one with God (about which we learn no more) and one with an angel, who weeps and asks for mercy. If this reading is correct, then the theological problem of God asking a human being for mercy would apparently also be resolved.[10]

But even if there are two traditions behind Hos. 12.4b-5a, both traditions have the same content: Jacob struggled with God. The מלאך that Jacob struggles with can hardly be anything other than a Yahweh-מלאך, and thereby a representative for Yahweh. We may still have the problem of 'the weeping God', but the question is: is it not in fact Jacob who weeps and begs for mercy in v. 5a? A. Bentzen draws a parallel between Jacob's weeping and praying and Moses' intercessory prayer for the people by means of 'mighty fasting and prayer' (Deut. 9.9–10, 11): 'Jacob uses all the usual ways of imploring God for blessing and conquers'.[11] If

---

10. A number of different attempts at a solution have been proposed, the majority with a point of departure in Gen. 32.23ff. Pedersen, *Israel*, III-IV, p. 504, claims that Gen. 32.23ff. describes a struggle between another god and Yahweh, and Hosea knew a similar story (pp. 516-17 note 1 to p. 505). Nyberg, *Studien*, pp. 94-95, makes a similar proposal. See also de Boer, 'Genesis XXXII₂₃₋₃₃', pp. 162-63. Wolff, *Hosea*, pp. 212-13, regards מלאך as a gloss, while אל is the subject for the root שרר: 'Thus Hosea says that he who acts deceptively, who cunningly fights against God and man, will encounter his Lord and victor in Yahweh…Jacob wept and made supplication because Yahweh had defeated him.' Thus also Jeremias, *Hosea*, p. 153.

11. Bentzen, 'The Weeping of Jacob, Hos XII₅ₐ'. Rudolph, *Hosea*, pp. 228-29, takes a different position: in Hos. 12.5a, he finds a special tradition (*Sondertradition*) that demonstrates that Jacob received his honorary name (*Ehrenname*) in a manner

this is the case, then Jacob's action must be perceived as the only possible one: the only way Jacob can deal with a representative of the mighty God in his struggle is to humiliate himself before him. C.T. Francisco[12] interprets the Jacob section in Hosea 12 as the story of a conversion that should serve as an example for Israel. According to Francisco, Israel was under the influence of the Canaanite cult, but nothing better could be expected of them, in that they were simply following their father Jacob, who in his youth wished to overcome every form of resistance. Francisco continues:

> Yet Jacob finally made his peace with God. Israel must not imitate the faults of Jacob without also seeing the challenge of his faith. He struggled against himself and God but won the battle by supplication.

Francisco's position is not without its faults, but he does point to an important aspect in the tradition of Jacob's struggle with God: it is precisely through the struggle that Jacob gains the blessing to live as God's elected. In this sense the traditions concerning Jacob have what are almost mythical traits. We thus find two abbreviated references to (presumably) two traditions, where Jacob either struggles with God or with his representative. The fact that Hosea does not provide a narrative development of these two traditions can once again be explained by assuming that they were known beforehand. We cannot know what shape and development the traditions have had, and an interpretation taking its point of departure exclusively in Gen. 32.23-33 must be regarded as methodologically uncertain. The etymology of the name and the motif of the struggle are common features of the two pericopes, and that is all that we can conclude on the basis of a comparison. In addition, it is probable that two traditions also lie behind the presently unified (*einheitliche*) story in Genesis.[13]

But there are also important *differences* between the two expositions. Surely the most important of these is that in Hosea there is no geographical localization of the Jacob struggles, whereas in Genesis פנים (Gen. 32.21-22, 31; 33.10), and thus Penuel, must be regarded as a

---

that is hardly flattering, namely, 'by means of weeping and supplication (*durch Weinen und Flehen*)'. Mays, *Hosea*, p. 163, and Good, 'Hosea and the Jacob Tradition', pp. 143-44, also speak of special traditions.

12. Francisco, 'Evil and Suffering in the Book of Hosea', pp. 34-35.

13. Blum, *Vätergeschichte*, pp. 143ff., argues against the traditional position regarding the separation of sources in Gen. 32.23ff.

leading word both within the pericope itself as well as in the context.[14] Von Rad has called attention to the compositional continuity between the theophany reports in Genesis (Gen. 28.10-15; 32.23-30).[15] Against this background E. Blum sees a connection between Bethel and Penuel, where Bethel legitimated Penuel as the seat of government for a short period during the reign af Jeroboam I. Blum's intention is to date the compositional layer of the Jacob story (Gen. 25B*; 27–33) to the period immediately following the division of the kingdom.[16] It would take us too far afield to argue here against this understanding. In any case, it is suggestive that such a linking together of Bethel and Penuel is to be found in Genesis. Does Hos. 12.5 show that Jacob's struggle once belonged to Bethel's cult legend?

Hosea 12.5b

בית־אל ימצאנו ושם ידבר עמנו

he met him at Bethel,
and there he spoke with him.

The two most significant problems in this half-verse are the understanding of בית־אל and the meaning of the verbal suffixes: are they first person plural or third masculine singular, and do they both have the same form?

Bethel can be understood either as a geographical name or as the name of the local deity, El-Bethel. This El-Bethel, who is also known from the Elephantine Papyri (cf. also Jer. 48.13), could have been worshipped in Bethel, and this state of affairs could thus be regarded as an explanation for the strong polemic against Bethel as a place of worship.[17] In relation to this issue, one could ask: why should Hosea

---

14. Thus already Gunkel, *Genesis*, p. 356. See in addition Blum, *Vätergeschichte*, p. 143.

15. G. von Rad, *Genesis*, 'Das erste Buch Mose—Genesis', p. 256.

16. Blum, *Vätergeschichte*, pp. 175-86.

17. This understanding of the situation has received its classic elaboration by I. Engnell, 'Hosea', *SBU*, I, col. 980, who states that El-Bethel 'in no way is the same god as Yahweh, even if the congregation at Bethel thought so'. Engnell translates Hos. 12.5 as follows: 'And he struggled with and conquered a god, who, while weeping, begged for mercy (for himself). This (god) is found in Bethel, and he speaks with us there'. In other words, El is found in Bethel, a pathetic god, whom Jacob had legitimated after he had conquered him at Jabbok. In addition, Gen. 35.7 and 31.13 are referred to in support of the existence of El-Bethel, but both of these

employ the place name Bethel, if he meant the god El-Bethel? And
further: in every other passage where Bethel is mentioned in the book of
Hosea (4.15; 5.8; 10.5)[18] it appears under the slanderous name בית און,
'house-of-evil'. Why is this not the case here, if the presumed purpose
should be a polemic against the cult at Bethel? And especially so, if the
root און is considered as one of the key words in Hosea 12.[19] Actually a
strong argument can be made for understanding Bethel as a place name
on the basis of its parallel position to the locative pronoun שם in 5ba.[20]
The two half-verses have in addition a clear parallel structure: specification of place[21]—verb (imperfect)—object. We can translate: At Bethel he
found him/us, there he speaks to him/us.

But who is represented by the object suffixes? Good sets forth the
eight possibilities for translating the words ימצאנו בית־אל.[22] If we choose
the most obvious possibility (which corresponds to the reading of the
Masoretes), the object in 5ba is Jacob. We are familiar with two traditions in Genesis about Jacob's meeting God in Bethel (Gen. 28.10-22;
35.9-15). Both of these stories must be regarded as literary composi-
tions,[23] which in the course of the narrative have been placed in a
transitional position for Jacob, namely, on the one hand, the transition
from the Jacob–Esau cycle to the Jacob–Laban cycle (Gen. 28.10-22)

passages must be regarded as rather uncertain examples for demonstrating a linkage
between Jacob and El-Bethel. In this regard, see J. Van Seters, 'The Religion of the
Patriarchs in Genesis', pp. 224-25.
    18. See, however, 10.15, where בית־אל should presumably be read בית־ישראל,
BHS b-b.
    19. See vv. 4, 9a (compare עון 9b), and 12; cf. Jeremias, *Hosea*, p. 149.
    20. For the problems concerning El-Bethel, see in addition Blum, *Vätergeschichte*,
pp. 186-90.
    21. For the *accusativus loci*, see Gesenius–Kautsch, §118d.g.
    22. Good, 'Hosea and the Jacob Tradition', p. 145:

    1)   At Beth-el, he (Jacob) finds him (God);
    2)   At Beth-el, he (God) finds him (Jacob);
    3)   At Beth-el, he (Jacob) finds us;
    4)   At Beth-el, he (God) finds us;
    5)   At Beth-el, one finds him (God) = At Beth-el he is to be found;
    6)   Beth-el (divine name) finds him (Jacob);
    7)   Beth-el finds us;
    8)   Beth-el, he (Jacob) finds him (Bethel).

    23. See in this regard R. Rendtorff, *Das überlieferungsgeschichtliche Problem
des Pentateuch*, pp. 40-65.

and, on the other hand, from the Jacob–Laban cycle back to the Jacob–Esau cycle (Gen. 35.9-15). From this we can deduce that (1) Bethel is seen to be a key place in Jacob's life, for Jacob and Bethel are closely connected to one another, and that (2) there are not necessarily two traditions behind the two Bethel sagas, but perhaps two aspects or theses of one tradition.

It is in other words a risky business to decide which of the two Jacob–Bethel narratives Hosea had in mind. The patriarchal reports, as we know them in Genesis today, had not received their final form at the time of Hosea, and it is in fact highly probable that Hosea is simply referring to a situation that was well known beforehand, namely that Yahweh revealed himself to Jacob at Bethel. This corresponds precisely to the use of the Jacob traditions that we have observed previously.

The suffix in 5bα is thus best understood as third masculine singular. Is this also the case for 5bβ? A number of versions claim so (cf. *BHSb*),[24] and the parallelism supports this reading. But the question is: does it make sense? And does not the unambiguous reading (עמו → עמנו) restrict our understanding of the sense of the verse? Good suggests that the suffixes in both of the partial verses be read with conscious ambiguity, as both 'him' and 'us', in that Good understands Jacob as a symbol for Israel and thus the word 'Jacob' can always be replaced with the word 'Israel'.[25] It would actually be more appropriate to say that there occurs a shift in meaning from 'Jacob' to 'Israel' in 12.5b. The significance of Jacob's history and his actions are set before the listeners, his descendents. In the course of v. 5b it is made clear that it was not only in the past that Jacob met Yahweh at Bethel, but that he also 'speaks to us' in the present (12.3).

So much for the figure of Jacob himself in Hos. 12.4-5. It would appear that a picture emerges that confirms Francisco's theory that Jacob should serve as an example of a conversion that is to be imitated by Israel: Jacob deceived his brother, fought with God and won, but afterwards begged for mercy and was found and spoken to at Bethel.[26]

---

24. Compare RSV.
25. Good, 'Hosea and the Jacob Tradition', pp. 140, 146.
26. M. Fishbane, *Biblical Interpretation in Ancient Israel*, pp. 376-78, finds in Hos. 12 what he depicts as *aggadic, typological exegesis*. Jacob is the *typos* of Israel: 'Hos. 12 applies events in the individual biography of Jacob to the nation as a whole...', Fishbane claims, portraying Jacob as the primordial transgressor. Jacob's *personal* activities were considered the typological antecedent for Israel's *national*

Hosea 12.6

ויהוה אלהי הצבאות יהוה זכרו

Yahweh the God of Hosts
Yahweh is his name

The understanding of this verse and its provenience is closely bound up with its function in the redactional context, to which we shall return below. Rudolph[27] understands vv. 6-7 as the content of what Yahweh says 'to us' (v. 5) and the words in v. 6 as 'the free creation of Hosea' (*freie Schöpfung Hoseas*). Wolff characterizes v. 6 as a doxology of judgment (*Gerichtsdoxologie*), which is known from Josh. 7.19, and he refers to the doxological insertions Amos 4.13b; 9.5-6, with which there is some agreement. At the same time he notes that it is impossible that the same redaction lies behind the doxologies in Hosea and Amos, in that the differences between the formulations in the two books are too great.[28]

I agree with T. Naumann that the verse is best characterized as a 'post-Hosean, doxological expansion'. Naumann adapts Crüsemann's characterization of the formula as originally a doxology that concludes a participial hymn.[29] The use of the formula in the book of Hosea is meanwhile atypical (*untypisch*), in that the formula has been detached from its original function. In terms of tradition history Naumann places the formula in this detached form in connection with the ark of the covenant in Jerusalem,[30] while chronologically the formula in its present

transgression and 'it would appear that for the prophet, in so far as the individual Jacob-Israel is the ancestor of Israel, his behaviour has to some degree *determined* the behaviour of his decendants [...]. The nation is not just 'like' its ancestor, says Hosea, but *is* its ancestor in fact—in name and in deed' (Fishbane's italics).

27. Rudolph, *Hosea*, pp. 229-30.
28. Wolff, *Hosea*, p. 213.
29. T. Naumann, *Hoseas Erben*, pp. 109-10.
30. T.N.D. Mettinger, 'YAHWEH SABAOTH', p. 134, demonstrates that there was quite likely a cult for יהוה צבאות in Shilo before the temple there was destroyed. No connection is seen between יהוה צבאות or אל צבאות and Bethel. On the contrary, it is likely that there was competition between the Cherub iconography in Shilo, which had a close connection with the whole complex of meaning around יהוה צבאות, and the bull iconography at Bethel (Mettinger refers here to F.M. Cross, *Canaanite Myth and Hebrew Epic*, pp. 198-215). It is unlikely that there was influence from the Shilo sanctuary, in that its temple is generally regarded to have lost whatever significance it might have had after the eleventh century. See, for example, I. Finkelstein, *The*

longer form belongs to the time of the exile.[31] According to Naumann, the striking use of זכרו instead of the more common שם is due to the doxology's liturgical background and its function of actualization.

Hosea 12.7

ואתה באלהיך תשוב
חסד ומשפט שמר וקוה אל-אלהיך תמיד

With your God's help, you shall return.
Hold fast to love and justice
put always hope in your God.

Only one question will be touched upon in this verse, namely the understanding of the verb שוב. This verb does not have any unambiguous meaning, but according to the context can be translated as 'return', 'come back' and 'convert'. Here in Hos. 12.7 the verb is normally translated 'return'[32] but nothing in the context necessitates such a translation. It is far more probable that the correct translation is 'turn back/convert'. The meaning of the pericope thereby becomes far clearer. The purpose of the indictment that Yahweh has against Israel (12.3; see pp. 43-46) is to bring the people of Israel to the point where they will convert.

Hosea 12.3-7: Form and Content

At this point in the exegesis redactional issues begin to be urgent. With regard to form, 12.3-7 in its present state is a unified whole. But who has put the pericope together and for what purpose?[33] We have observed

Archaeology of the *Israelite Settlement*, p. 232.

31. For the detailed argument see Naumann, *Hoseas Erben*, pp. 109-13.

32. *Zurückkehren, revenir*; it is presumably this understanding of the Hebrew word that has resulted in the emendation of באלהיך to באהליך (*BHSa*). Ackroyd, 'Hosea and Jacob', pp. 252-53 understands v. 7 as a call to return to the semi-nomadic life for which Jacob is an example (*typos*).

33. One could certainly make the legitimate claim that such questions are meaningless: the text provides excellent kerygmatic and theological meaning, the dissolution of the text into several component parts does not increase our understanding of the text, it is not possible to isolate the *ipsissima verba* of the prophet, such redactional investigations are encumbered with all too many possibilities for error, and so forth. On the other hand, it would appear meaningless to conduct an investigation if the wish to get to the bottom of a problem is at the outset rejected as illegitimate. The discussion has become more and more prevalent in recent years, but the skepticism mentioned has been expressed previously by Engnell, *Gamla Testamentet*, I, *passim*. See in addition Good, 'The Composition of Hosea', p. 57.

a linguistic connection between v. 3 and vv. 4-5 (see above, n. 3). There are two possible explanations for this. Verses 3-5 could be a unit from Hosea or the Hosea tradition itself, and then v. 7 must belong to the original unit. If it does not, then the pericope, as we have seen, does not have a conclusion and is without meaning. Verses 3-5 cannot stand alone. On the other hand, the possibility must be considered that v. 3 has been created on the basis of the wordplays in vv. 4-5, and that in this way the Jacob pericope has been made into a building block within a later context. If this is the case, then vv. 3, 6 and 7 are secondary additions, either prior to or simultaneous with the final composition of Hosea 12. The first possibility remains, however, the most likely: vv. 3-5, 7 originally belonged together (see below).

We have identified redactional measures in vv. 3 and 6. The change of the addressee in v. 3a, where the original 'Israel' has been changed to 'Judah', is a Judaean redaction, which Naumann dates to the late pre-exilic period and places in Judaean prophetic circles that preached judgment (*unheilprophetische Kreise*).[34] Verse 6 has been dated to the exilic period.[35] It cannot be definitively determined as to whether the correction in v. 3 took place before or simultaneously with the specification in v. 6.

The redactional measures that have taken place in vv. 3 and 6 have nevertheless not caused any substantive changes in the pericope. Both must be regarded as attempts to make the message more precise. Hos. 12.6 explains who is the subject of the verbs in v. 5b, or, in other words, who the true God in Bethel is. At the same time, the verse makes clear who is the God who speaks in v. 7. God in Bethel is יהוה אלהי הצבאות.[36] We

---

34. Naumann, *Hoseas Erben*, 109.

35. In this connection see Emmerson, *Hosea*, pp. 63ff. Emmerson claims that the change is a meaningful reappropriation of the oracle after the fall of Samaria, where Judah remained as the sole inheritor of the name Jacob and the old traditions concerning the people of God, but this does not mean that the change cannot be as late as the period of the exile, where the pan-Israelite point of view was also prevalent in the Deuteronomistic movement.

36. Thus also Naumann, *Hoseas Erben*, p. 115. The Bethel legends are in Genesis also the legends of the holy places of the Yahweh cult. Rudolph notes (*Hosea*, p. 229 n. 19) that v. 6 contradicts the perception that the pericope should be understood as a polemic against the god of Bethel as an idol, which is argued for, among others, by de Boer, 'Genesis XXXII$_{23-33}$', pp. 162-63, and Ginsberg, 'Hosea's Ephraim', pp. 343ff. See in addition Ackroyd, 'Hosea and Jacob', pp. 256-57.

can, therefore, without reservation include vv. 3 and 6 in the exegesis of the passage. What the tradition had gathered before the Judaean redaction existed as meaningful speech, which did not require essential changes.

Verse 7 interprets the *télos* of the pericope for us: with the help of Yahweh, the God of Hosts, you—Israel—must return with חסד and משׁפט, faithfulness and justice, two concepts that are central for Hosean theology (see below, Chapter Three). The purpose of the indictment that Yahweh has against Israel (12.3) is to make Israel convert. The verse may well have been understood in this way by the exilic redaction as well, which inserted v. 6; but the meaning 'return home' had presumably at that time also swung in the direction of the understanding of שׁוב in v. 7.

The Theological Context of Hosea 12.3-7
If we look more closely at the pericope in its present form, it is important to note that it is introduced with a so-called *rîb*-expression (v. 3). Still, 12.3-7 cannot be placed within a *rîb*-pattern.[37] Nevertheless, there can be no doubt that the text is an accusation against Israel because of its actions. This is emphasized in v. 3b, where the verbs פקד and שׁוב (hif.) both have the meaning of retribution. In other words, Yahweh will enter into a lawsuit with his people: this is the introduction to the Jacob pericope, and it is from this point of view that the pericope must be read. But, at the same time, the 'superscription' in v. 3 cannot be detached from the conclusion of the pericope in v. 7, for in this verse it is stated what Yahweh intends with this lawsuit, namely, to help the people to return to the true cult, which once was in Bethel (see v. 6).[38]

This form for a saving lawsuit or punishment is found several places in the book of Hosea. The *locus classicus* is the great divorce trial in

37. On the concept of *rîb*-pattern, see K. Nielsen, *Yahweh as Prosecutor and Judge*, pp. 23-26.
38. The context of a common content is supported by an observation with regard to form, namely that vv. 3 and 7 have the same structure, where three verbs mutually correspond, not in form, but in breadth of meaning:

	v. 3		v. 7
	ריב		שׁוב
	פקד		שׁמר
	שׁוב		קוה (pi.)

This observation further points to the possibility that the same author is responsible for both verses.

Hos. 2.4-17.[39] The introduction is made with the proclamation of a trial, the witnesses are called, the guilt of the accused is substantiated, and the justice and inevitability of the punishment are set forth. It should be noted that the verb פקד in this context appears in 2.15 [MT], which sums up the metaphor of the preceding verses and speaks directly about the real offences:

> I will punish (ופקדתי) her for the festival days of the Baals,
> when she offered incense to them
> and decked herself with her ring and jewelry,
> and went after her lovers,
> and forgot me, says Yahweh.

But after the proclamation of the terrible punishment (vv. 8-15) it turns out that the punishment is a purification that will effectuate the catharsis that is the presupposition of the re-establishment of the proper relationship between God and Israel.[40] The proper relationship is the one that existed at the time of Israel's youth, when God brought her up from Egypt, before the fall at Achor.[41] The lawsuit that is proclaimed in 2.4 has led to restoration and not to condemnation, in spite of the demonstration of the sin of the accused.

Such is also the case in 12.3-7. The indictment that begins as a threat (12.3) turns out to be an occasion for conversion (v. 7a), not on the basis of Israel's own efforts, but with the help of Yahweh, the God of Hosts. There is, however, a significant difference between the lawsuit in 2.4-17

39. For a more detailed analysis, see Wolff, *Hosea*, pp. 30-45; K. Nielsen, *Yahweh as Prosecutor and Judge*, pp. 34-38; D.J.A. Clines, 'Hosea 2: Structure and Interpretation'. These scholars all claim that the pericope is a unified whole. On the other hand, there is some disagreement as to whether, and to what degree, it is a genuine (divorce-) trial.

40. A different understanding is set forth by Clines, 'Hosea 2: Structure and Interpretation', who sees in the pericope an expression of Yahweh's considerations concerning his relationship to the faithless people. There are three possibilities, of which the first two are rejected by Yahweh, namely, 'imprisonment (vv. 8-10) and deprivation (vv. 11-15)', while he decides for the third possibility: 'restoration (vv. 16-17)'. Clines himself is well aware of the improbability of such indecisiveness on the part of God, but he maintains that in other passages as well Hosea intimates that God struggles with himself (6.4; 11.8). In addition, he refers (p. 87) in this connection to Wolff, *Hosea*, p. 119.

41. We see here yet another example of how Hosea simply alludes to an 'event' in Israel's past without expanding upon it. It might be the event known from Josh. 7.24-26 (cf. Wolff, *Hosea*, p. 43).

and the pericope in 12.3-7. In 2.4-17 both the crime and the punishment are described with the use of powerful images. We do not find such an exposition in 12.3-7. After the proclamation that Yahweh will punish Jacob for his deeds, we are presented with a review of the Jacob traditions. But these must be regarded as indirect accusations against Israel. Jacob is depicted as the highly gifted person who believed in Yahweh at precisely the moment that Yahweh appeared to be weak (5a). Ackroyd expresses it as follows:

> Is it not more likely that he is saying: 'The success of your father Jacob was due to divine favour, and to the closeness of relationship which was his with God?'[42]

Jacob struggled successfully with both human beings and God (4-5aα), but he did not thereby become arrogant (5aβ). In Bethel he was found[43] by God, the very God who also *there* speaks to present-day Israel: Yahweh, the God of Hosts (5b-6).

In all probability the two *rîb*-passages have been composed by the same author-redactor, who chronologically precedes the Judaean redaction. It is, of course, also possible that one of the *rîb*-statements provides the point of departure in terms of form for the other, but if this is the case, then it is not possible on the basis of what is given to determine which of the two statements is the oldest. One would then have to decide which of the two parts of the book of Hosea (chs. 1–3; 4–14) was first put together.[44]

In 12.3-7 Yahweh makes use of the same pedagogical method as in 2.16-17, where he tries to reason with Israel in the desert. Here again it is Yahweh's intention to show Israel the proper way to go, and this is

---

42. Ackroyd, 'Hosea and Jacob', p. 258. The objections of Vollmer, *Geschichtliche Rückblicke*, pp. 111-12 n. 302, which are based on literary-critical arguments, are not convincing.

43. The verb מצא is employed in other places in the book of Hosea about Israel, who is found by God. R. Bach, 'Die Erwählung Israels in der Wüste', maintains that a special prophetic tradition is to be found, in which Yahweh found Israel in the desert (the so-called finding tradition, *Fundtradition*), and that this tradition must be understood as an Election tradition. Bach does not, however, speak of the Jacob traditions in this connection. Concerning the tradition that Israel was found in the wilderness, see Chapters 3 and 5, below.

44. This is due to the fact that the pericope 2.4-17 (MT) must be regarded as the point of departure for the composition of Hos. 1–3 (cf. Good, 'The Composition of Hosea', pp. 28ff.).

the way that Jacob followed. This way will certainly bring them back to the true cult in Bethel, as opposed to the false cult, which everywhere else in the book of Hosea is referred to by the name Bet-awen.[45] God will help the people of Israel to convert, so that they can again live in harmony with the demands of a proper relationship to God. That Yahweh's assistance is necessary for conversion to take place comes clearly to expression in other passages in the book of Hosea (see, for example, 11.8-11; 12.2-4). Indeed, one can understand this form for God's healing love as a characteristic feature of Hosea's theology.[46]

Israel in the Wilderness: Hosea 12.10-11

Hosea 12.10 is understood by Wolff and other scholars as a threat (*Drohwort*).[47] Wolff does indeed consider the possibility that there is a connection between life in the tents and the feast days, which is also pre-supposed in 9.5-6, but he does believe, however, that it is more probable that Hosea is thinking of Yahweh's first meeting with Israel in the desert (9.10; 2.5; 10.11).[48] Precisely for this reason it seems obvious to me to regard 12.10-11 as a promise to re-establish the old relationship, which, as noted previously, also is the case in 2.16-17 (which Wolff also refers to).[49] I shall examine 12.10-11 more closely in Chapter 3, and I shall, therefore, only maintain by way of anticipation that this pericope can also be understood in a positive fashion.

---

45. Emmerson, *Hosea*, pp. 124-38, argues that Hosea did *not* have a hostile relationship to the cult in Bethel, but only to the abuse of the cult. The prohibitions in 4.5 should thus not be understood as destructive of the cult, but their function is to protect the cult against the apostate people (as opposed to Wolff, *Dodekapropheton*, I, p. 89). Indeed, the context (4.14b-19; cf. Good, 'The Composition of Hosea', p. 35) deals with the apostasy of the people and their fate. Correspondingly, 10.5 is directed against the calf idol. At the same time, Emmerson finds evidence for the idea that 'Bethel is not Bethaven but Yahweh's house' (133; cf. 8.1; 9.4, 8; 10.5). The reading *bêt ʾāwen* is a tendentious vocalization of *bet ʿôn*, which is another name for Bethel.

46. Wolff, *Hosea*, p. xxix.

47. See, among others, Rudolph, *Hosea*, p. 234, and Naumann, *Hoseas Erben*, p. 114.

48. Wolff, *Hosea*, p. 215.

49. Compare כימי מועד in 12.10 with כימי נעוריה in 2.17.

Jacob and the Prophet: Hosea 12.13-14

ויברח יעקב שדה ארם ויעבד ישראל באשה ובאשה שמר
ובנביא העלה יהוה את־ישראל ממצרים ובנביא נשמר

Jacob fled to the land of Aram,
there Israel served for a wife,
and for a wife he guarded sheep.
By a prophet Yahweh brought Israel up from Egypt,
and by a prophet he was guarded.

These two verses constitute a semantic, formal and kerygmatic unit.[50] Many regard them as a condemnation of Jacob—and thereby of the people. The mention of the prophet (who usually is identified as Moses) in v. 14 supports this condemnation, in that he is seen to be the diametrical opposite of Jacob. If one's perception of the picture of Jacob in 12.4-5 is negative, then this will also be the case in 12.13[51]. On the other hand, if one has (as do H.-D. Neef and P.R. Ackroyd) a positive view of the picture of Jacob in 12.3-5, then one also has a positive view of Jacob later on in the chapter. One can thus choose to consider v. 13 and v. 14 either as polar contrasts or as supplementing each another.

The verses supplement one another. The key word in vv. 13-14 is שמר. Just as Jacob once—after he fled—guarded sheep for his father-in-law, so has God guarded Israel with the help of a prophet.[52] Verse 13 refers to traditions that were alredy well-known about Israel's father, Jacob: he fled to Aram and became a shepherd in order to earn a wife for himself. The allusion is rather abbreviated—a technique, which, as

---

50. See, for example, H.-D. Neef, *Heilstraditionen*, pp. 52-53.

51. Typical of the negative perception of the relationship between Jacob and Moses is the view of E. Jacob, 'Der Prophet Hosea und die Geschichte', p. 286: 'the one lives for the sake of a woman…the other is a prophet, i.e., he lives for the sake of the word, he is not the servant of a woman, but of God'. See in addition Rudolph, *Hosea*, pp. 230-31; Vriezen, 'La Tradition de Jacob dans Osée XII', pp. 75-76; Wolff, *Hosea*, p. 216. It is incomprehensible that there should be, as Wolff writes, something degrading about earning the sum necessary to purchase the bride by working for his father-in-law. In addition, the word עבד is not synonomous with 'slaving (*Sklavendienst zu leisten*)'. Finally, there is no indication that the verse is in fact dealing with the participation of the patriarchs and the people in sexual rites of some sort.

52. One could add: …after he had let him lead them as a flock up from Egypt.

we have seen, is characteristic for the use of traditions in the book of Hosea.

Along with this tradition we find a similarly abbreviated mention of a prophet, who led Israel up from Egypt. The prophet does not have a name, but for the most part scholars agree that the prophet is Moses. The fact that the name is not mentioned is, however, striking, especially since Jacob is called by name in v. 13.[53] There are several possible explanations for this state of affairs. Perhaps the prophet is not Moses at all. One could surmise that there existed a tradition in which Yahweh had brought Israel up from Egypt with the assistance of a prophet, who was not identified as Moses. In other passages (for example 11.1) Hosea also presents an understanding of the Exodus that does not mention Moses. It is, in fact, first at a much later time that Moses acquires his totally dominating role.[54]

Another possible explanation can be found in the message of the verse: it is not the *person* of Moses that is the most important issue but rather the emphasis on the task of the *prophet*. He is a guide, and he is a guardian (ובנביא נשמר)—as was Jacob. This is the same prophetic role that is described in 9.8 and that lies behind the description of the ideal period in 12.10-11.

My understanding of the relationship between Jacob and Moses is close to that of Ackroyd, who writes that

> Hosea is offering an interpretation of the servitude of Jacob as in some way equivalent to Israel's servitude in Egypt—in other words not a matter of Israel's failure but a situation which provided the occasion for a divine act of salvation.[55]

In other words, it would appear that the mention of Israel's past refers back to the time in which it had the proper relationship to God. This

---

53. But see Wolff, *Hosea*, p. 216.

54. See in this regard, H. Schmid, *Die Gestalt des Mose*.

55. Ackroyd, 'Hosea and Jacob', p. 247. Ackroyd bases his understanding on the parallelism with the so-called Historical Creed in Deut. 26.5-9. The argument made against Ackroyd by Good, 'Hosea and the Jacob Tradition', p. 149, must be rejected. When Good draws parallels between Jacob's servitude for the purpose of purchasing a wife and other passages in the book of Hosea, where the purchase of a prostitute or whore is spoken of in more or less metaphorical terms (4.10, 12-15; 8.9; 9.1), he fails to see the difference between the purchase of a bride and sheer prostitution. At the same time, he fails to see the difference between allusions to a saga and the use of metaphors.

corresponds to the understanding found in other passages in the book of Hosea. We refer again to the 'classical' passage, Hos. 2.17b: 'There she shall respond as in the days of her youth, as at the time when she came out of the land of Egypt'. Similar expressions are to be found in, for example, 9.10; 11.1; 13.4. In all these passages a mention of how Israel deserted Yahweh after the period of her youth follows a positive expression about the original relationship between Yahweh and Israel.

Something similar can be observed in Hosea 12, where we have already seen how negative expressions follow positive ones (vv. 10-11 + 12 and vv. 13-14 + 15).[56] This observation has, of course, implications for the understanding of the redaction of the book of Hosea.

The Redaction of Hosea 12

Verses 1-2 form the introduction to the third section of the book of Hosea, chs. 12–14, just as 4.1-3 formed the introduction to the second major portion of the book, chs. 4–14. A *rîb*-statement in v. 3 follows 12.1-2, just as was the case in 4.4 following 4.1-3, and while this *rîb*-statement is a call for conversion, it is seen in v. 15 that the *rîb* leads to punishment. The preaching of conversion is first resumed in 14.2, and personal conversion is there combined with the promise of 12.10b-11 that Yahweh himself will act to bring about salvation. At the same time 12.10-11 cannot be separated from its immediate context, Hosea 12. This is evident because of the 'zig-zag' structure that we already have found in Hosea 12 and because one of the chapter's key themes, deceit, is already presented in v. 1.[57]

The exegetical investigations have confirmed the observation that I made in the beginning of this chapter, namely, that the references to Israel's past were positive, while the mention made to the present situation was negative. It has not been possible to decide definitively the provenience of the individual positive statements, but the bulk of the evidence suggests that Hosean thinking lies behind such statements. We have been especially interested in vv. 3-7, and we have found here a theology of conversion that corresponds to what we have found in other passages in the book of Hosea. We may assume, therefore, that this

56. Compare the understanding of Gese, 'Jacob und Mose: Hosea 12.3-14 als einheitlicher Text', p. 47.

57. Naumann, *Hoseas Erben*, p. 101. An opposing view is found in Daniels, *Hosea and Salvation History*, p. 39.

constitutes a genuine portion of the Hosea tradition that has been passed on by the 'Hosea disciples'.

Various aspects of ancient Israel's history with God are pointed out in sharp contrast to Ephraim's present conduct. Ephraim deceives, just like his ancestor, Jacob. In contrast to Jacob and the previous generations, Ephraim participates in the sinful cult, and, if we include the introduction in vv. 1-2, he makes treaties with Assyria and Egypt in contrast to the Israel that Yahweh let a prophet lead up from Egypt.

As has been demonstrated, the past is described in a positive fashion.[58] There is, however, a difference in the picture presented in v. 10 (which leads up to an act of salvation on the part of Yahweh in v. 11) and vv. 13-14, on the one hand, and that presented in vv. 3-7, on the other hand, which does not operate with a harmonic golden age, but on the contrary with the conversion of the patriarch as an example for Israel.

Is there a *Tendenz* in Hosea 12 that makes it possible to determine with a fair amount of confidence the existence of a single, late redactional layer? Hardly. It is not possible to discern the existence of a special Deuteronomistic 'tone' or of a 'tone' that indicates that the return is near.[59] On the other hand, we cannot prove that all of the material—or even part of it—originates with Hosea himself. But the basic thrust of the entire chapter does indicate the pre-Judaean period, and that means at the very least the disciples of Hosea. We are dealing with a compositional unit that has been cleverly put together and where it is necessary to use the exegetical scalpel in just a few places. Hosea 12 is clearly marked by literary, compilational activity. It has been rightly described as 'an artful network of mutual references, allusions, and catchword-connections'.[60]

We have already discussed the presence of Judaean redactional activity in connection with the alteration of an original *Israel* to *Judah* in v. 3. It is presumably the same hand that lies behind the later reinterpretation (*Nachinterpretation*) that is found in 12.1b: '...but Judah still walks with God, and is faithful to the Holy One'. It cannot be definitively decided as

---

58. Correspondingly, 13.4; see below, Chapter 3.

59. As opposed to Yee, *Composition and Tradition*, pp. 229-48. She regards 12.1a, 2-4, 8-9, 13, 15 as a portion of the earliest Hosean tradition, while 12.1b, 5-7, 10, 12, 14 have been shaped by the so-called R2, an exilic-Deuteronomistic redactor.

60. '...ein kunstvolles Netz gegenseitiger Bezugnahmen, Anspielungen und Stichwortverbindungen'. See further Naumann, *Hoseas Erben*, pp. 100-102.

to whether or not 12.1b in its entirety is secondary. But the correction in v. 3 indicates that 'Judah' in 12.1b can have displaced a previous subject that we are not in a position to reconstruct. The verse contains significant philogical and exegetical problems. I follow Naumann, who after an exegetical examination concludes that the content of the verse is negative, that a Judaean tradent has brought Hosea's message up to date and that this tradent can be found in those circles that preached judgment prior to the destruction of Jerusalem.[61] He also finds the work of these circles in other passages in the book of Hosea.

One can thus conclude that Hosea reuses known traditions that he interprets. Early tradents (or redactors, if one wishes) have gathered these late Hosean reinterpretations (*Nachinterpretationen*) and placed them in a context of exhortation that was brought to Judah and first here found their final form as we know them today.

---

61. Naumann, *Hoseas Erben*, pp. 104-107.

Chapter 3

ISRAEL—YAHWEH'S REBELLIOUS PEOPLE

A. *Covenant—Election*

Israel is the people of Yahweh's possession. This is a fact of fundamental significance for the entire Old Testament exposition, regardless of whether it is understood as salvation history or as the history of a disaster. But Yahweh's possession is a rebellious one, and the Old Testament does not contain any accounts about how Yahweh shares a perfectly happy existence with this possession. On the contrary, Israel's apostasy is in one way or another a conspicuous feature of a large portion of the Old Testament. All this is obvious.

What is not so obvious, however, is the question about *how*, according to the Old Testament, Israel became the people of Yahweh's possession. The Old Testament itself has various explanations of how this came about, explanations that are in mutual competition with each other. But this should not be surprising. It is a commonplace that the same state of affairs can be presented in different ways. This is also the case for the book of Hosea. The fact that Israel is Yahweh's possession is expressed by the use of different metaphors. Israel is Yahweh's wife (Hos. 1–3), he found Israel in the desert (9.10-15; 13.5-6), he saw her beauty and skill (10.11-13a), he called her from Egypt (11.1; 12.10 [MT]; 13.4), and he chose Jacob (12.5). On the other hand, Hosea does not speak of a covenant agreement as somehow being fundamental for the 'possession relationship'.[1] This perception of the situation, however, has not always been the prevailing one in the field. On the contrary, the concept of the covenant

---

1.   'Possession relationship' is a translation of the Danish word *ejendomsforhold*. This section is based upon my article, 'דעת אלהים und חסד im Buche Hosea', where there is also documentation for the claims made here. The views set forth here have in addition taken the works of E.W. Nicholson, *God and his People*, and J. Day, 'Pre-Deuteronomic Allusions to the Covenant in Hosea and Psalm LXXVIII', into consideration.

has been regarded as fundamental for the book of Hosea, as has also been the case for the understanding of Old Testament theology as a whole.

The Question of Covenant Theology

H.W. Wolff in the 1960s elaborated the 'classic' understanding of Hosea's theology.[2] He sees in the concept of the covenant a demand for the recognition and confession of Yahweh's deeds for Israel, a demand that was established in the Yahweh-covenant of the tribes of Israel in the period between the sojourn in Egypt and the settlement.[3] Theology, דעת אלהים, is *covenantal* theology. Correspondingly, חסד is the same as covenantal loyalty (*Bundestreue*), and צדקה/צדק is the same as covenantal law (*Bundesrecht*).[4]

L. Perlitt's monograph, *Bundestheologie im Alten Testament* (1969), raised major problems for Old Testament scholars as far as this understanding of Hosea's theology as covenantal theology is concerned—as well as for the understanding of the covenant in many other respects.[5] Perlitt explains the so-called covenantal silence (*Bundesschweigen*) in the early writing prophets (which has greatly puzzled exegetes) by arguing that the covenant simply did not exist as a theological concept prior to the Deuteronomic movement. The emergence of covenantal theology is closely connected with the emergence of the Deuteronomic movement, ברית is a Deuteronomic *theologumenon*, and covenantal theology does not, therefore, form the background for Hosea's theology. In those passages in the book of Hosea where the word ברית is found (2.20; 6.7; 8.1; 10.4; 12.2) it is not a question of the Sinaitic covenant, with the exception of 8.1, which is a Deuteronomistic gloss. Hosea does not require a covenantal theology in order to express what he means about Israel's relationship to Yahweh. Yahweh's demand upon Israel does not have its foundation in the Sinaitic covenant, but in a legal claim that is grounded in the history in which Yahweh led Israel out of Egypt (for example 13.4). When Hosea deplores Israel's apostasy, he does not speak about a breach of the covenantal relationship, but about adultery. Hosea has not been influenced by the Deuteronomic/Deuteronomistic covenantal

---

2. See 'Hoseas geistige Heimat' and 'Wissen um Gott als Urform von Theologie', as well as *Hosea*.

3. Wolff, 'Wissen um Gott', p. 199.

4. See Wolff, *Hosea*, p. 180, for the translation of Hos. 10.12, and cf. 'Wissen um Gott', *passim*.

5. For the following see Perlitt, *Bundestheologie im Alten Testament*, pp. 129-55.

theology, but the situation is rather the reverse: the marriage parable of Hosea 1–3 has played a role in the formation of the Deuteronomistic covenantal theology. With his marriage parable (*Ehegleichnis*), Hosea belongs to the 'background' of covenantal theology.[6]

ברית is, therefore, not a key theological concept in the book of Hosea in the way it is for the Deuteronomists and the Deuteronomistic writers. But how is the concept then employed? Perlitt's interpretation is in fact quite convincing. The perception that the theology of the book of Hosea is a decidedly covenantal theology appears to a great degree to have been inspired by the 'knowledge' that familiarity with the Deuteronomic/Deuteronomistic theology has given us. But is it correct to exclude covenantal thinking completely from the book of Hosea? Is Perlitt's notion that the marriage metaphor is fundamental to the theology of the book of Hosea possibly dependent upon a tendency in the research rather than upon the text itself?[7]

The two passages where ברית is spoken of are Hos. 6.7 and 8.1. In order to understand these two verses, it is necessary to consider them together. If 8.1b is Deuteronomistic, as Perlitt believes it to be, then it is natural to interpret 6.7 in the light of the marriage metaphor and therefore not as an expression of covenantal theology. On the other hand, if one views 6.7 as a legitimate expression of Hosean covenantal theology, then Perlitt's understanding of 8.1b is not quite so compelling.

Hosea 6.7; 8.1b: Exegesis
The genuineness of Hos. 6.7 is not questioned by Perlitt, and this is, therefore, a good place to begin the investigation.

והמה [8]כאדם עברו ברית שם בגדו בי

> But at Adam they transgressed the covenant;
> there they dealt faithlessly with me.

The two sections of the verse are parallel, that is to say, the verbs עבר and בגד are parallel, whereby it follows that the covenant that is the object for עבר is a covenant with Yahweh.[9] But the book of Hosea does

---

6. If Perlitt is right, it is necessary to reflect again concerning the meaning of the concepts חסד and צדק/צדקה in the book of Hosea. See further in this regard Excursus 2 below, pp. 91-93.

7. With regard to this problem, see Jeremias, *Hosea*, p. 7.

8. Reading with *BHSb*, as has been customary since Wellhausen.

9. This is further supported by the parallelism between the place name אדם and the locative pronoun שם.

not have a rigorous understanding of what this covenant implies. It is not a question of some kind of תורה[10] or of any particular covenantal agreement. As far as the mention of the covenant is concerned, the historical events of the Exodus and the period in the wilderness, which the Deuteronomistic formation of the tradition associates with it, are not referred to, although they are otherwise recurring themes.[11] The covenant that the book of Hosea speaks of cannot be identified with the Deuteronomic/Deuteronomistic covenant, but it must be understood, however, in the light of its theology as a whole.

The covenant is just one way of illustrating Yahweh's demand. Far more important than the terminology involved is the meaning of the term, and for Hosea and the Hosean tradition what is fundamental is faithfulness to Yahweh. This faithfulness can be depicted in many ways, by means of the marriage metaphor, the categories of fertility, and the traditions about Yahweh's election of Israel—or described as a covenant. This covenant is not depicted in the light of the Sinaitic covenant, but as a contrast to other, already known *political* treaties. Moreover, this corresponds structurally to the book of Hosea's depiction of the proper Yahweh cult as a contrast to the popular cultivation of Baal.

If Hos. 6.7 is authentic, then 8.1b may be as well.

יען עברו בריתי ועל־תורתי פשעו

because they have broken my covenant
and transgressed my law.

The terminology of the verse is not quite as foreign to the book of Hosea as Perlitt believes. J. Day has, for example, called attention to the use of the expression עבר ברית (8.1b) in both verses and to the fact that the expression ועל־תורתי פשעו is not found in the Deuteronomistic literature.[12] The most important aspect of Perlitt's argument is certainly the parallelism of תורה and ברית, which he claims first makes its appearance in the Deuteronomistic literature. But the fact that a terminological feature is typical for one literary form does not methodologically exclude

---

10. *Contra* Nicholson, *God and his People*, pp. 184-85.

11. I am not in agreement with Nicholson's argument for the presence here of a covenantal theology similar to that of the Deuteronomist; cf. *God and his People*, pp. 183-86.

12. J. Day, 'Pre-Deuteronomic Allusions', p. 7; cf. Nicholson, *God and his People*, p. 186.

the possibility that other, perhaps earlier, texts can exhibit the same feature without it necessarily being a gloss. In other words, there is no methodological reason to exclude the possibility that Hosea can independently have used this grouping, but he did not make use of it in the paradigmatic fashion that we find in the Deuteronomistic literature.[13]

The book of Hosea is familiar with the word תורה with a non-Deuteronomistic meaning (cf. 8.12), and the parallel between תורה and ברית is moreover in agreement with the use of תורה made by the early writing prophets. The parallel use of the two words does not, therefore, convincingly demonstrate that 8.1b is Deuteronomistic. On the contrary, a good explanation can be given as to why Hosea or the Hosean tradition made use of the collocation *before* it became formalized.

Returning to the word ברית, which Hosea alone among the eighth-century prophets makes use of,[14] we have already observed with Perlitt how Hosea employs the term in a way that is significantly different from the Deuteronomic/Deuteronomistic use of the word. Hosea employs the term in its 'original' sense, which is concerned with political treaties (12.2; 10.4), and he also uses the term in reference to the covenant of peace that Yahweh will conclude—not with Israel, but for the sake of what is best for Israel (2.20). But, at the same time, in 6.7 we have seen that Hosea *can* speak about a covenant with Yahweh. Accordingly, it does not have to be foreign in 8.1b.

Yahweh's Demand for Exclusivity
The paralleling of תורה and ברית can support Perlitt's and Zimmerli's understanding of the relationship between Israel and Yahweh as a legal one. If, in fact, we adhere to Wolff's understanding of דעת אלהים, knowledge of God or theology, as a demand for an open recognition of Yahweh's historic right to Israel and as a demand that the people be informed of this legal claim by the priests, the תורה in the book of Hosea

13.   On the other hand, I cannot agree with Day, 'Pre-Deuteronomic Allusions', pp. 8-12, when he claims that Ps. 78.10, 37 is an example of a pre-Deuteronomistic use of the comparison between law and covenant. The dating of this Psalm to the period prior to 722 BCE is highly disputed, which Day also admits. For a more thorough treatment and argument, see my article, 'דעת אלהים und חסד im Buche Hosea', especially pp. 90-97. The issue is thoroughly discussed by J. Jensen, *The Use of tôrâ by Isaiah*.

14.   The word does not appear in either Amos nor Micah. The singular instance כרתנו ברית את מות in Isa. 28.15 corresponds in usage precisely to that made in Hosea; cf. also Perlitt, *Bundestheologie*, pp. 135-39.

is another word for this instruction, and ברית is another word for Yahweh's demand. Following Zimmerli we will call this demand Yahweh's *demand for exclusivity (Ausschliesslichkeitsanspruch)*. In what follows it will be my claim that this demand for exclusivity is the essential feature of the theology of the book of Hosea.

Yahweh's demand for exclusivity is, in the Old Testament exposition, historically based upon his election of the people. As mentioned previously, the book of Hosea tells about this election by using different metaphors or forms. These forms of election do not appear to be mutually exclusive. In addition, none of them appears to have given the desired result, namely, that Israel remain faithful to Yahweh. In what follows we shall investigate the different traditions about Yahweh's election of his people in the book of Hosea in order to see whether there is any relationship to other traditions concerning Yahweh's election in the Old Testament. The Jacob traditions were discussed in the previous chapter, and the story of Hosea's marriage does not pertain to the focus of the present study, in that the marriage story does not make any specific mention of the election but presupposes it. The remaining traditions concerning the election are those of the people called from Egypt, the people found in the wilderness, and the people as the threshing heifer.

I have called these traditions *historical*. This does not mean, of course, that they can be regarded as historically reliable sources in any modern sense. On the other hand, they cannot simply be regarded as *mythological*. The book of Hosea operates with a 'historical' understanding of God, or in any case with an understanding that the election was a historical event. Therefore, in the following considerations concerning the connections between the Hosean tradition and other 'historical' traditions, it is not a question of delineating the 'historical' facts but of tracking the influence of the history of the tradition.

B. *The People Chosen in Egypt*

The assertion that Yahweh chose Israel to be his people already in Egypt is found in Hos. 11.1, 12.10a (MT) and 13.4a. The latter two passages have the same wording, while 11.1 differs from them by providing an expanded account. We will, therefore, in what follows first discuss these verses separately and afterwards compare the use made of the different statements.

Hosea 11.1

Hosea 1.1-11 is naturally delimited both with regard to what precedes
and to what follows, and v. 1 is the superscription of this unit.[15]

כי נער ישראל ואהבהו וממצרים קראתי לבני

When Israel was a child, I loved him,
and out of Egypt I called my son

The metaphorical language in the chapter is taken from the sphere of
family life,[16] of which the repeated theme in the chapter is Yahweh's
fatherly love and mercy towards his sons, a kind of mercy that goes far
beyond human mercy (v. 9). It is quite likely that the chapter has been
put together by a redactor,[17] but this is not a decisive issue for our

15.   Most scholars regard Hos. 11.10 or portions of it as a later gloss (for
example Wolff, Mays, Jeremias and Rudolph), while opinion is divided as to what
extent the chapter is to be regarded as an original unit or as a redactional collection.
16.   W. Schlisske, *Gottessöhne und Gottessohn im Alten Testament*, pp. 116-34
and pp. 175-76, arrives at a similar conclusion, in that he also rejects the influence of a
mythological background and refers instead to the wisdom tradition. He distinguishes
the use of the son metaphor in Hos. 11 from its use in Hos. 2, behind which lies the
mythological perception of the God who fertilizes the earth (in the shape of a
goddess). Schlisske is of the opinion that the royal ideology belongs in an entirely
different mythological context (cf. 2. Teil, pp. 78-115).
17.   Wolff, *Hosea*, p. 193-94, regards v. 1 as an introduction to the pericope
11.1-7, which he interprets as a version of the traditions about Israel's election in the
wilderness (cf. Neef, *Heilstraditionen*, pp. 87-88). In this regard, it is necessary to
make some textual adjustments in v. 2, where—in order that Yahweh can be regarded
as the subject of the verb קרא—כקראי is read with the LXX (*BHSa*). כן in v. 2a
requires that the כ be placed at the beginning of the sentence, and a temporal
subordinate clause of one kind or another is thereby read. At the same time, *BHSb* is
to be followed, whereupon הם at the close of 2a is connected to the beginning of 2b,
and the following is read:

כן הלכו מפני
הם לבעלם יזבחו

The revocalization of מפניהם → מפני הם is necessary; cf. Rudolph, *Hosea*, p. 209:
'The emphatic הם corresponds to the emphatic ואנכי in v. 3 ...' In this way, an
opposition between Yahweh and the people is set forth, which corresponds precisely
to the situation in 2.10. The first emendation, however, is to rejected as unnecessary.
קראו להם can be understood as an impersonal construction, whose subject is
understood to be the Baals or their priests; cf. Bach, 'Erwählung', 65 n. 76. We may
therefore translate:

'They called upon them,
thus they abandoned me.

purposes. In any case, the chapter is a kerygmatic unit, and it is introduced by a title that sums up its message.[18] In this superscription the
author refers back to the tradition of the call out of Egypt. The immense
importance of this tradition for the Hosean tradition is seen not only in
the passages where the event is mentioned directly (11.1; 12.10a;
13.4a),[19] but also by the fact that Israel's apostasy—as is also the case in
other places in the Old Testament—can be described as the voluntary
return of the people to Egypt (7.11; 12.2). On the other hand, the
punishment of the people means that they will be *sent back* to Egypt
(8.13; 9.3; 11.5), and Egypt can act as Yahweh's instrument of punishment (7.16; 9.6). In 11.11 a renewed return from Egypt is promised.[20]
In agreement with what we have observed concerning the Jacob traditions in Chapter 2, we do not find in 11.1a comprehensive presentation
of the tradition to which reference is being made. There is no mention
made of great and marvellous deeds, of the prophet who led the people
(12.14), of the obedience of the people (2.17), or of their disobedience.
Mention is only made of a theme: Yahweh has called Israel, his son, at
the time of his youth in Egypt.

The depiction of Israel as a youth (נער) is first found in the Old
Testament in the book of Hosea; the image is employed later by
Jeremiah (2.2; 3.4). The word has a number of different layers of
meaning, but in this context it must be understood as an expression for a

> They sacrificed to the Baals,
> burned incense to idols.
> Yet it was I...

In conformity with Hosea's point of view in other passages, 11.2-7 describes the
apostasy as a recurring event. It is not a question here of a 'primal fall', but of
Ephraim's continuous association with idols, as it thus comes to expression in v. 7.
Hos. 11.2, 7 can therefore, in agreement with Wolff, *Hosea*, p. 193, be characterized
as an historico-theological accusation (*eine Geschichtstheologische Anklagerede*).
We are not here within the realm of mythology, but within the sphere of דעת אלהים,
the theological tradition of knowledge. Israel's apostasy is not spoken of here by
means of mythological metaphors but directly.

18. Cf. for example, the superscription to the book's second main section, Hos.
4.1-3, and to section 4.4-10, 4.4.

19. 2.17 and 12.14 also play upon this tradition.

20. See in this regard Wolff, *Hosea*, pp. 202-203. In a number of the passages
mentioned Egypt appears together with or parallel to Assyria (7.11; 9.3; 11.5, 11; 12.2).

youthful age, without the attribution of any special quality.[21] The specific reference to the time of the occurrence, כי נער, indicates that it was long ago that Yahweh began to love Israel. There is no attempt made to play upon Israel's obedience in its youthful period as was the case in 2.17. The two passages are quite different in their use of metaphor. In 2.17 Israel is spoken of as Yahweh's youthful lover, while 11.1 remains within the realm of childhood: Israel became Yahweh's son, not his wife or betrothed. While 2.17 speaks of the time after the election, 11.1 refers to the period preceding the call and to the call itself.[22] The structure of the verse indicates that נער and בני are parallel, and that election and love are one and the same thing. For Hosea love is the interpretative key to election.[23]

Hos. 11.1 would appear to be a purely 'historical' statement about the first election, free from any other mythological motifs, but part and parcel of the tradition of knowledge, דעת אלהים, in accordance with which Hosea demands that Israel must live. The statement stands forth as something fundamental to this tradition of knowledge, for it provides the framework of understanding for what follows. Without any sense of contradiction, the call out of Egypt and the election in the wilderness are spoken of in the same breath.[24]

In Hosea 11 the call out of Egypt is not followed by apostasy, but it forms the background for all of the later elections. Wolff is certainly correct when he speaks of 'Israel's original creed' (*Urbekenntnis*

---

21.   Wolff, *Hosea*, p. 1971: 'If the word in v. 11 is supposed to denote something more than the time of Israel's beginning, at the most it would refer to his helplessness (vv. 3-4 and 2.4), but in no way to his usefulness (as in 9.10; 10.11). The first event in the life of young Israel worthy of report is that Yahweh loves him.'

22.   The pericope 2.1-3 ought not to be included as parallel material, in that it must be regarded as a later addition: see Jeremias, *Hosea*, pp. 34ff., and Herrmann, *Heilserwartungen*, p. 117 n. 39 (against, however, the consensus of current research). If there is a question of dependence, then it is 2.1-3 that is dependent on 11.1 and not the other way around. There is, however, a connection between 2.1-3 and Hos. 3.

23.   Wolff, *Hosea*, pp. 197-98. Wolff's claim, *ibid.*, that Hosea should have employed the father–son relationship as an interpretation of a received conception of the covenant, must be deemed unlikely. The covenantal idea does not play a decisive role in the book of Hosea: cf. Holt, 'דעת אלהים und חסד im Buche Hosea', pp. 89-98.

24.   We shall later observe how Hosea can operate with a concept of election in the promised land itself.

Israels).[25] This understanding is strengthened by the investigation of the
other passages where the election is mentioned.

Hosea 12.10a (MT); 13.4a

While Hos. 11.1 speaks metaphorically about Yahweh's election of
Israel, in 12.10a and 13.4a we find a statement that speaks directly about
this election:

ואנכי יהוה אלהיך מארץ מצרים

> I have been Yahweh, your God,
> ever since the land of Egypt.

What is the tradition history of this expression?

Zimmerli calls the expression a 'formula of self-presentation'
(*Selbstvorstellungsformel*).[26] This divine formula of self-presentation is
often employed in priestly contexts (the Holiness Code, Ezekiel), either
in a shorter (אני יהוה) or in a longer form (אני יהוה אלהיך). In addition,
the formula is found in the introduction to the Decalogue (Exod. 20.2;
Deut. 5.6), and it is richly represented in Deutero-Isaiah. As is the case
here in the book of Hosea, the formula is often expanded by the use of
predicates and relative sentences, which emphasize one or another of
Yahweh's deeds for Israel. The formula is versatile (*beweglich*) and open
to interpretation (*interpretierbar*).[27] The formula has a cultic *Sitz-
im-Leben*, whereas it does not belong in a prophetic context. Hosea
is the only one of the older writing prophets who employs the self-
presentation formula, but this does not mean that it is necessarily an
interpolation when found in the book of Hosea or that it has been
'copied' from the Decalogue.[28] (The) Hosea (tradents) have presumably

25.   Wolff, *Hosea*, p. 197. An informative comparison might be Christian
baptism as the point of departure for every Christian's relationship to God.

26.   Zimmerli, 'Ich bin Jahwe', p. 14.

27.   Zimmerli, 'Ich bin Jahwe', p. 15.

28.   The question of Hosea's relationship to the Decalogue, which is raised in
particular by the accusations in Hos. 4.2, is dealt with by scholarship in the following
ways: (1) Hosea was familiar with the Decalogue and was able to include it in his
proclamation: Weiser, *Hosea*, p. 42; Mays, *Hosea*, 64; Rudolph, *Hosea*, p. 101;
Wolff, 'Wissen um Gott', pp. 194-95; (2) Some scholars urge caution and reservation concerning the issue: Wellhausen, *Die kleinen Propheten*, p. 109; Sellin, *Das
Zwölfprophetenbuch*, p. 39, speaks of collections that resemble the Decalogue; thus
also Crüsemann, *Bewahrung der Freiheit*, p. 24; (3) Some scholars see Hosea as the
presupposition for the Decalogue: Marti, *Das Dodekapropheton*, p. 39; Hossfeld,

taken over the formula from the cult.[29]

That the self-presentation formula is not bound up with the Decalogue or with its earlier stages, but must rather be understood as an independent expression, which can be connected to different conceptions, can be seen among other things from the fact that in 12.10a and 13.4a the formula is not placed within a 'decalogical' context.[30] It is connected in both passages to ideas surrounding a stay in the wilderness: 13.4b-6 refers to the time in the wilderness when Yahweh chose his people, but where they also rebelled,[31] while 12.10b-11 looks forward to a time of renewed salvation.[32] Just as was the case in 11.1, the relationship between Yahweh and Israel in Egypt is without problems. In Egypt there is no indication of any disobedience. In this regard 11.1, 12.10a and 13.4a correspond with 2.17, which can be understood as an expanded variation of the same *dictum*.

Results

If we again consider Hos. 11.1, 12.10a (MT) and 13.4a together, we can see that the election in Egypt in all three passages has the same function, namely as an introduction or title to other traditions, with which it has been unproblematically joined. Hos. 11.2-7 and 13.5-6 are both traditions about the election; 11.2-7 deals with the recurring call,

---

Der Dekalog, p. 277; Levin, *Die Verheissung des neuen Bundes*, pp. 91-92. Concerning the problem, see in addition Neef, *Heilstraditionen*, pp. 175ff.

29.   Expanding Wolff's ideas concerning a 'federation' between prophetic and Levitical circles in the Northern Kingdom, which stood in opposition to the ruling royal house and the priesthood ('Hoseas geistige Heimat'), one could imagine that the self-presentation formula was handed down in such circles. But Wolff's understanding must be tempered by the fact that Hosea cannot be said to be as hostile to the cult as Wolff and others suppose: see in this regard p. 46 n. 45, and Chapter 4.

30.   We have observed a similar chronological and temporal independence of a later literarily and theologically fixed concept in the use of ברית and תורה (see above, pp. 53-57). It is hardly obvious, as claimed by Neef, *Heilstraditionen*, p. 192, that Hos. 13.4 should follow after decalogue material, namely the prohibition of images. 13.2 does not prohibit making an image of Yahweh, but on the contrary it condemns the worship of other images of gods. Moreover, the rhetorical unit 13.1-3 (see Wolff, *Hosea*, p. 222) has a closer relationship to 12.1-15 than to 13.4, which does not continue 13.1-3, but forms the solemn introduction to 13.4-8.

31.   With good reason this election is not set forth as a covenant ratification; see pp. 50-57 above.

32.   Thus Herrmann, *Heilserwartungen*, pp. 116-67 with n. 38, contra Wolff, *Hosea*, p. 215.

which is followed by recurring apostasy (see p. 58 n. 17). Hos. 13.5-6 is concerned with the election in the wilderness, which will be discussed in the next section.

Hos. 12.10b-11 (MT) speaks of a stay in the wilderness (as does 13.5-6), not of a past but of a future stay that will be repeated in the days of the feast. In the wilderness Yahweh will guide his people through the prophets (12.11). A number of questions are raised by this pericope: what period of time is the text speaking of? Which prophets? And is it a question of a threat or a promise? The attempt has been made to find behind the words ימי מועד (the days of the festival) *either* a contemporary festival, such as the seven days of the feast of booths (Keil) or the Passover feast (Wellhausen) *or* a past nomadic feast of tents (Kraus).[33] Wolff notes that in Hosea statements about the future (כימי and כיום) always employ analogies from Israel's past (2.5, 17; 9.9; cf. 10.9), and that כימי מועד belongs to the tradition about Yahweh's first encounter with Israel.[34]

In continuation of these considerations, it would be appropriate to compare 12.10b with 2.17, כימי נעוריה. In both passages a new stay in the wilderness is mentioned. It is there that Yahweh will speak to the people as in the days of their youth or during the days of 'the feast'. An interpretation along these lines presupposes that 12.10-11 is understood to be a promise of a new beginning and not as a threat of punishment. Such an interpretation also presupposes that v. 11 is best read as a future tense rather than a past tense.[35] Hos. 2.16-17 and 12.10-11 are best understood with Fohrer as what one might call a cathartic pedagogy:

> Israel will be removed from her surroundings, which have destroyed her original relationship to God, so that she once again can come to her senses.[36]

Or one can follow Herrmann's interpretation:

33.   See in addition Neef, *Heilstraditionen*, p. 112.

34.   Wolff, *Hosea*, p. 215.

35.   Against Wolff, *Hosea*, p. 207 and p. 215), where he speaks of 'the threat made in 10b of a new nomadic situation', and translates 12.11 in the past tense: 'Hosea is probably thinking of the line of prophets in the Northern Kingdom... They are active still in Hosea's time, as the transition from the perfect verbs in v. 11a to the iterative imperfect in v. 11b suggests'. Cf. as well Rudolph, *Hosea*, pp. 234-35. But for the grammatical problems at issue see Herrmann, *Heilserwartungen*, p. 116 n. 37.

36.   G. Fohrer, 'Umkehr und Erlösung beim Propheten Hosea', p. 117, and cf. above pp. 45ff.

The time together with Yahweh in the wilderness is the prototypical
relationship to Yahweh in the classical period, a relationship never again
attained since the early period. It is here set before the people of Israel as a
new possibility.[37]

These two interpretations can supplement each other: Israel is to be
removed from the unfortunate influence of the surrounding culture[38]
and brought into the same situation as in the past, when she was obedi-
ent to Yahweh. She will there be able—after the cleansing—to choose a
new beginning.[39] Hos. 12.10-11 thus speaks about two 'beginnings', the
one in Egypt and the other in the wilderness. The mention of the
election in Egypt somehow implies the period in the wilderness,[40] and
the combination of the two different 'beginnings' takes place without
creating major problems. This reinforces the view that the 'call from
Egypt' functions as a 'primeval event'.

The question thus remains: how did this tradition originate? At the present time there are quite a number of opinions. The theory that prevailed
until just a few years ago—that a number of tribes did, in fact, emigrate
from Egypt and then settled in the area of the northern tribes[41]—has in
recent years been called into question by the sociological understanding
of how Israel arose, namely as the result of either a revolution (the
school of Mendenhall) or an evolution (Lemche) in Palestine itself.[42] It
would take us too far afield to dwell upon these theories, and the
possible historicity of the Exodus events is irrelevant in the present

---

37.   Herrmann, *Heilserwartungen*, p. 116.
38.   It is, however, not a question of some kind of nomadic ideal: see Neef,
Heilstraditionen, p. 113.
39.   Cf. also Sellin, *Das Zwölfprophetenbuch*, p. 124: 'It is thus a question of
precisely the same ideas as i 2.16, not about the realisation of the Rechabite ideal in
Palestine, and it is a question about the proclamation of a punishment that leads to an
improvement, to salvation, which is clearly shown by v. 11'.
40.   Cf. Sellin, *ibid.*; and cf. Herrmann, *Heilserwartungen*, pp. 116-17, who
understands the entire unit as reflecting a redactional process: 'One has thus to
recognize in 12.10-11 an originally independent traditional passage that has been
inserted here, a passage whose originally positive aspect has been darkened in the
present context and now appears to demand a different understanding'.
41.   The 'classical' monograph in this regard is—as in so many other cases—
Noth, *Geschichte Israels*. This point of view has also been maintained in some
recent histories of Israel as, for example, S. Herrmann, *Geschichte Israels in
alttestamentlicher Zeit*.
42.   The sociological theories are discussed in detail in Lemche, *Early Israel*.

context. It is sufficient to observe that the tradition about Egypt is also fundamental for the Hosean tradition. It is impossible to discern how much of this tradition contained historical-narrative material, in that the Pentateuchal narratives in their written form are from a later period. As to what the book of Hosea tells us concerning the election in or from Egypt, we can sum up as follows: Yahweh called the people of Israel from Egypt in the earliest age, and Israel followed him obediently, when Yahweh led them up with the help of a prophet. Hosea found it necessary to tell so much—or so little—about Israel's beginning. We cannot know whether or not he or his contemporaries 'knew' more, but there can be no doubt that this knowledge of Israel's beginning was central. We find ourselves here at the very heart of the conception of דעת אלהים in the book of Hosea.

C. *A People, Called in the Wilderness*

Grapes in the Wilderness: Hosea 9.10-17

Form, Textual and Tradition Criticism

10 Like grapes in the wilderness,
I found Israel
Like the first fruit on the fig tree, in its first season
I saw your ancestors
But they came to Baal-peor,
and consecrated themselves to a thing of shame,
and became detestable like the thing they loved.

11 Ephraim's glory shall fly away like a bird—
no birth, no pregnancy, no conception!

12 Even if they bring up children, I will bereave them until no one is left.
Woe to them indeed when I depart from them!

13 Ephraim, whom I once chose as a young palm, planted in a meadow
Ephraim must now lead out his children for slaughter.[43]

14 Give them, O Yahweh—what will you give?
Give them a miscarrying womb and dry breasts.

15 Every evil of theirs began at Gilgal;
there I came to hate them.
Because of the wickedness of their deeds
I will drive them out of my house.
I will love them no more; all their officials are rebels.

---

43. Differently NRSV; cf. below p. 70 with nn. 61-63.

16 Ephraim is stricken, their root is dried up,
    they shall bear no fruit.
    Even though they give birth,
    I will kill the cherished offspring of their womb.
17 Because they have not listened to him,
    my God will reject them;
    they shall become wanderers among the nations.

Hos. 9.10-17 is usually understood as a kerygmatic unit, consisting of two parallel constructed oracles of judgment, 10b-14 and 15-17, which have been joined together with a common title in v. 10b.[44] The pericope does not appear to have been through more than one redaction, and Wolff's view that it was written down in its present form by a group of Hosea's disciples is quite probable, in spite of the premises for his reasoning.[45] But this is not an argument for the original unity of the pericope—not even along with form-critical observations.[46] Indeed, it is hardly meaningful to discuss the existence of something 'original' before the writing down of this passage, for it is impossible to go behind the written material. It is, finally, totally unrealistic to make conjectures about the existence of a manuscript written by the prophet himself.[47]

The point of the pericope is clear: after the election in the wilderness[48]

---

44. Wolff, *Hosea*, p. 162; Neef, *Heilstraditionen*, 68-69. A different understanding is found, for example, in Rudolph, *Hosea*, pp. 180ff., who understands Hosea's prayer in v. 14 as an interruption and does not regard vv. 15-17 as the original continuation of vv. 10-13. The context is redactional. Verse 16 has been incorrectly put into place (late, and for mechanical reasons), and the verses originally had the following sequence: 10, 16a, 11, 16b, 12-14. As already mentioned, vv. 15-17 are redactional additions.

45. Cf. Wolff, *Hosea*, p. 163.

46. Cf. Jeremias, *Hosea*, p. 121.

47. *Contra* Rudolph, *Hosea*, p. 187.

48. There has been some discussion as to whether במדבר is connected to מצאתי or to ענבים, that is to say, as to whether it is a question of a tradition where Yahweh finds Israel in the wilderness or whether 'the wilderness' is an aspect of what is marvellous about the grapes. Grapes in the wilderness and the first fruit on the fig tree are both something unusually delightful, and the probability of finding grapes in the wilderness has been considered by for example Sellin, *Das Zwölfprophetenbuch*, p. 76, and Rudolph, *Hosea*, p. 185. Bach's perception that the metaphor and the thing itself—as so often in Hebrew—are one and the same is the most probable understanding. This view is also supported by Rudolph, *Hosea*, p. 185, although he most decidedly rejects the idea that Israel had any inherent value, and moreover totally rejects Bach's theory concerning a special finding tradition.

(cf. אבותיכם in 10aβ), the people rebelled (vv. 10b and 15a) and they must now, therefore, suffer the consequences, namely annihilation (the children must be killed) and rejection. Hos. 9.10-17 is the introduction to a part of the book of Hosea (9.10-14.2) that repeatedly makes use of historical retrospections in order to place the present situation in relief. The mention of the time in the wilderness in 9.10a is the natural point of departure:

כענבים במדבר מצאתי ישראל
כבכורה בתאנה בראשיתה ראיתי אבותיכם

Like the grapes in the wilderness, I found Israel.
Like the first fruit on the fig tree, in its first season
I saw your ancestors.

This half verse is in fact the point of departure for R. Bach's thesis concerning a special finding tradition (*Fundtradition*) that contradicts the tradition received in the Pentateuch.[49] The verse consists of two parallel members, 10aα and 10aβ, and deals with Yahweh's election of Israel. The verbs מצא and ראה are parallel and should thus be understood together. Rudolph (inspired by Ehrlich and Sellin) understands them as an expression for 'the subjective perception (*das subjektive Empfinden*), that is, 'how do you find it?',[50] while a majority of commentators follow Bach in understanding that מצא—and thereby also ראה—here means elect[51] without, however, all accepting the idea of a finding tradition.

After this introduction there are two oracles that deal with the apostasy of the people and the ensuing punishment. According to 9.10b, the apostasy took place at Baal-peor. The events that Hosea refers to here are usually understood to be identical with those that are mentioned in Num. 25.1-5, even though Baal-peor is not a place name elsewhere in the Old Testament but is the name of a god who dwells in that place. As usual, the allusions are scanty, and one would do well in any case to avoid supposing that there is some kind of *literary* dependence. There is no reason to believe that Hosea should have read Num. 25.1-5 or have known a corresponding story. Nothing speaks against the possibility, however, that he could have been familiar with an oral tradition that lies behind the present report.[52]

49. We will return to Bach's thesis and the reactions to it in Chapter 4.
50. Cf. Judg. 9.26; Rudolph, *Hosea*, p. 185.
51. Cf. Hos. 12.5; Deut. 32.10; Pss. 89.21; 132.5, 13.
52. Bach, 'Erwählung', p. 16.

For these reasons—and due to the fact that Num. 25.1-5 has, in addition, been transmitted incompletely,[53] reworked by the Deutero-nomistic writers,[54] and is difficult to place within the chronology of the Pentateuchal traditions—it is not possible to use the context surrounding Num. 25.1-5 to make a precise determination about the 'chronology' and the content of the apostasy mentioned. In other words, we cannot assume with Bach that Hosea has had the time of the occupation of the land in mind,[55] and we also cannot know the form of the apostasy in question.

Hos. 9.15 mentions the apostasy of the people at Gilgal, an apostasy that was so egregious that it called forth Yahweh's hatred:

כל-רעתם בגלגל כי־שם שנאתים
על רע מעלליהם מביתי אגרשם
לא אוסף אהבתם כל־שריהם סררים

Every evil of theirs began at Gilgal;
there I came to hate them.
Because of the wickedness of their deeds
I will drive them out of my house.
I will love them no more;
all their officials are rebels.

The play on words concerning the rebelliousness of the officials, כל-שריהם סררים, could indicate that political disparities were in mind, and the reference to the evil at Gilgal in v. 15a could point in the same direction. But is it a question of apostasy in the past or in the present? The second possibility is preferred by Rudolph: Hosea is speaking here as in 5.1-7, 6.7-10 and 7.3-9 about 'events of the recent past...that were common knowledge'.[56] Others claim that 9.15a refers to the coronation of Saul (1 Sam. 11.15).[57] In this connection, it is possible to speak about precisely the election of this king as an expression of defection from Yahweh—a good Deuteronomistic way of thinking (see, for example, 1 Sam. 8; 10.17-27).

53.   Noth, *Überlieferung des Pentateuch*, p. 81.

54.   S. Lehming, 'Versuch zu Ex XXXII', pp. 30-31.

55.   Bach,'Erwählung', pp. 16-17; cf. also Neef, *Heilstraditionen*, p. 75: '...although Israel was already faithless in its first contact with the cultivated land'.

56.   It is, moreover, according to Rudolph, *Hosea*, p. 188, uncertain as to which Gilgal is in question.

57.   See, for example, Wolff, *Hosea*, p. 167; Jeremias, *Hosea*, p. 124; E. Jacob, 'Der Prophet Hosea und die Geschichte', p. 284.

At the same time the majority of scholars believe that it is also a question here of *cultic* apostasy, and that Hosea here—as in other places—deals with cultic practices and politics as two sides of the same coin (cf., for example, Hos. 8). This possibility is not on the face of it improbable, but two objections can be made:

First, it cannot be assumed that the report in 1 Samuel 11 concerning the choice of Saul as king was common knowledge for Hosea's audience—or for the prophet and his disciples themselves, for that matter. In 1 Samuel we have no less than three traditions about Saul's election to the kingship (1 Sam. 9.1–10.16; 10.17-27; 11). In addition, we cannot assume *a priori* that a northern prophet would participate in the condemnation of Saul's kingship that we find in the Deuteronomistic History. Indeed, one could in fact be tempted to believe that in the Northern Kingdom one would have had a more sympathetic view of Saul, who was not a Judaean. Moreover, it is doubtful if Hosea would have shared in such a resistance to the monarchy in principle (cf. 5.1a), although the prophet clearly dissociated himself from the kings of his time.

Secondly, the other references to Gilgal in the book of Hosea are related to cultic situations (4.15; 12.12),[58] and the rest of v. 15 has a 'cultic' content. In 12.12aβb we have a closer description of the defection from Yahweh in Gilgal:

> In Gilgal they sacrifice bulls
> so their altars shall be like stone heaps
> on the furrows of the field.

Unfortunately, there is a problem for our understanding of the passage, namely, that the sacrifices of bulls was not an offence—on the contrary! We can only make guesses as to what the sin involved amounted to,[59] but there can be no doubt that it is a question of a cultic offence. The evil of Gilgal is of a *purely cultic* character,[60] and the punishment consists therefore in expulsion from the shrine. It is not stated directly as

---

58. Cf. Hos. 5.1-2, where what the leaders are guilty of is also called rebellion against Yahweh; see Mays, *Hosea*, p. 136.

59. See Emmerson, *Hosea*, pp. 139ff., for a closer account of the suggested corrections that have been inspired by this problem and their implications for interpretation.

60. This is also the view of N. Lohfink, 'Hate and Love in Hosea 9,15', p. 417, although he calls the sin committed at Gilgal 'a sin in the political realm'. He regards it as being 'a disturbance of the loyalty relationship between Yahweh and his people', contained in 'covenant love'.

to when this evil manifested itself, but perhaps the same situation is in mind as in 12.12, and that means that present conditions are involved. If this is the case, then we have in 9.15 a description of how the apostasy has continued and continues. Central to the understanding of the pericope 9.10-17 and its structure is the obscure v. 13a:

אפרים כאשר־ראיתי לצור שתולה בנוה61

What does this mean? Rudolph has proposed the simplest solution: he retains the portion of the text that is understandable and focuses his attention on the one obscure part, namely לצור. צור has been understood by the Peshitta, the Targum, the Vulgate, and Luther to be the name of the city Tyre, but what can be expected in connection with שתולה, planted, is the name of a plant. The best suggestion is to be found— without a textual correction—in the Arabic word *sawr*, 'palm seedling, young palm'.[62] The translation thus becomes:

> Ephraim, whom I once chose
> as a young palm, planted in a meadow.[63]

It is thereby evident that v. 13 presents a contradiction between past and future.[64] This fact is emphasized by the repetition of Ephraim and by the use of ראיתי which must be seen in the light of ראיתי in v. 10: v. 13 also describes an election in the past.[65]

With regard to the structure of Hos. 9.10-17, we can thus observe that, while there is no reference to the past in v. 15, there are two such references in vv. 10-14. These two references formally resemble each other more than is the case for vv. 10 and 15. Both in vv. 10 and 13 we find first a mention of the election and then a description of the apostasy, while only the last item is found in v. 15. It is therefore likely

---

61.   Sellin, *Das Zwölfprophetenbuch*, p. 77, translates the received text: 'As I saw it planted as a Tyrus in the meadow', and regards it, moreover, as 'sheer nonsense'. Today a translation is often cited based on LXX (*BHS b-b*): 'Ephraim, as I see, has exposed his sons to the hunt'. See Wolff, *Hosea*, pp. 160-61; thus also Neef, *Heilstraditionen*, pp. 66-67; Mays, *Hosea*, p. 131.

62.   This suggestion was already set forth in *Blumen althebraischer Dichtkunst* (ed. C.W. Justi; Giessen, 1809), pp. 536ff.

63.   Rudolph, *Hosea*, pp. 180ff.: 'Ephraim, das ich <mir vormals> ersah, / als junge Palme, auf eine Aue eingepflantzt'; and cf. Jeremias, *Hosea*, p. 119.

64.   Rudolph, *Hosea*; Jeremias *Hosea*, p. 123.

65.   Rudolph, *Hosea*; Jeremias, *Hosea*.

that 9.10-17 is not an original unit, but that vv. 15-17 is loosely attached to vv. 10-14. Verses 15-17 consists of two parts, v. 15 and vv. 16-17. There is no necessary connection between vv. 15 and 16.[66] Verse 15 unquestionably forms a whole, of which the description of sin and the punishment for it forms a part—the structure corresponds precisely to 10.9-10. As far as the composition is concerned, vv. 16-17 can be placed as a transitional member between 9.10–14.15 and 10.1, in that in v. 16 we find both allusions to the punishment (the death of the children) in vv. 11-13 and to the image of the vine plant in 10.1. Verse 17 must thereby be regarded as the interpretation of the images.

Interpretation

Let us now return to the theme in question, Hosea's election theology. In 9.10-14 we have delimited two statements about Yahweh's election of Israel, v. 10a and v. 13a. There does not seem to be any doubt that the two verses have the same presupposition (as does also 10.11-12; see below, pp. 77-97), namely, that Yahweh chose beautiful Israel for himself. Both verses employ metaphors from the plant kingdom that describe what is beautiful, lovely and fertile. But both verses continue by describing how Israel—or Ephraim— lapsed, how the good and chosen people became perverted.

The cause for this appears most clearly in v. 10b, which reproduces the tradition of the apostasy at Baal-peor, where the fathers dedicated themselves, וינזרו, to shame, לבשת, a rewriting of the divine name בעל.[67] According to Rudolph, there is a bitter irony to be found in the choice of the verb נזר: 'the Nazirite (*nazir*) binds himself to certain commitments in order to prove himself to be a faithful follower of Yahweh (Num. 6; Amos 2.11-12)'.[68] The consequences of devotion to Baal are the opposite of what was desired, namely the extinction of the ancestors instead

---

66. This is implied by Rudolph's suggestions about rearrangements; see above, p. 66 n. 44.

67. The reason the god is called הבשת is most likely to be explained by Hosea's wish to employ synonyms in parallelism: see Wolff, *Hosea*, p. 165. Hosea is the first to employ this rewriting, but we find it again in Jer. 3.24; 11.13 along with the pejorative rendering of the names ירבשת 2 Sam. 11.21 = ירבעל Judg. 6.32 and אישבשת 2 Sam. 2.8 = אשבעל 1 Chron. 8.33. Moreover, Hosea employs the root בוש in connection with precisely this issue: 2.7; 4.19; 10.6.

68. Rudolph, *Hosea*, p. 185.

of fruitfulness.[69] This will occur when Yahweh abandons them, v. 12b. This dreadful threat is summed up in v. 13: Ephraim, who at the time of the election was so fruitful, has now been the cause of his own collective suicide.[70] The pericope concludes with the prophet's prayer to Yahweh to carry out this decision (v. 14). It has been said that out of compassion for his countrymen Hosea asks God to 'be content with' the least horrible punishment.[71] Childlessness is to be preferred to war and the destruction of Israel. Wolff writes, 'It is as though Hosea, like David in 2 Sam. 12.12ff., chooses the punishment in which Israel yet remains in Yahweh's hand'.[72] However attractive this thought might be—and notwithstanding the fact that v. 14 bears the impress of Hosea's struggle with himself and his God—it is, however, more likely that the terrible prayer for 'a miscarrying womb and dry breasts' is the final summation of the preceding verses' proclamation of punishment.[73] Verse 13 states that this judgment is already at work. Yet another example of Israel's disobedience in v. 15 is added to the statement about the continued apostasy throughout Israel's history with Yahweh, and vv. 16-17 sum up the merciless conclusion: Ephraim, the beautiful plant, must perish; the chosen people will be rejected by its God.

69.   The utter obliteration is depicted with the help of a stylistic figure, the so-called unreal synchoresis (*irreale Synkorese*: H. Gese, 'Kleine Beiträge zum Verständnis des Amosbuches', pp. 436-37). According to Western thinking, it would appear to be an illogical device, but at the same time it presents a powerful poetic depiction of the extent of the catastrophe. Everyone will be wiped out, and even if there should—contrary to any reasonable expectation—be anyone left over, they too will be annihilated (cf. Amos 9.1).

70.   The nature of this self-inflicted murder of the children, which will entail the destruction of the nation, is not indicated. In general commentators envisage the events of the Syro-Ephraimite war or one of the wars with Assyria during the last ten years of the Northern Kingdom. Once again we see how cultic and political issues are interwoven in Hosea's understanding.

71.   See, for example, Wolff, *Hosea*, pp. 166-67; Rudolph, *Hosea*, p. 187; and cf. the considerations in J. Lindblom, *Prophecy in Ancient Israel*, pp. 204-205.

72.   Wolff, *Hosea*, p. 167.

73.   Sellin changes his mind in the second and third editions of his commentary in *Das Zwölfprophetenbuch*. In the first edition v. 14 was understood as 'a scream, which throughout corresponds to Hosea's disposition. He begs for the mildest form of punishment, that of v. 11: not to be born at all' (p. 77). In the second and third editions he writes: 'Hosea's prayer does not restrict the divine threat; on the contrary, it simply emphasizes it . . . ' (p. 99).

Hos. 9.10-17 is an oracle of judgment that has its point of departure in
election theology. By the use of rich metaphors the chosen people's
original lovableness is described at the time they were found and chosen
in the wilderness. As long as the subject is the election, the terminology
is metaphorical-mythical and not historical. When the apostasy is
described, the terminology is, however, concrete-historical. The diffi-
culties we encounter when trying to explain what exactly is under
discussion are due to the techniques of intimation and abbreviation that
we have previously touched upon as characteristic of the transmission of
the book of Hosea. Hos. 9.10-17 describes the mythical fact *that* the
beautiful Israel was chosen by Yahweh, not the historical *how*.

Yahweh's Flock: Hosea 13.5-8
Text
Hos. 13.5-8 also refers to the call or the election in the wilderness. This
time the metaphors are taken from the animal kingdom and not the
plant kingdom, as was the case with 9.10-17. Israel is described as a
flock that grazes and is satiated but forgets Yahweh. Yahweh will therefore become like the wild animals, who kill the flock. The election
account is introduced by the cultic self-presentation formula, 13.4.[74]

5   It was I who fed you in the wilderness
    in the land of drought.
6   When I fed them, they were satisfied;
    they were satisfied, and their heart was proud;
    therefore they forgot me.
7   So I will become like a lion to them,
    like a leopard I will lurk beside the way.
8   I will fall upon them like a bear robbed of her cubs,
    and will tear open the covering of their heart;
    there I will devour them like a lion,
    as a wild animal would mangle them.

The primeval election takes place in Egypt (v. 4a). The self-presentation
is followed by an emphasis on Yahweh's demand for exclusivity (v. 4b).
Verse 5 gives the reason for the imperative that resides in the demand
for exclusivity by referring to the election in the wilderness:

אני ידעתיך במדבר

With the support of LXX, Wolff changes ידעתיך to רעתיך.[75] This correction

---

74.   See above, pp. 57-65.
75.   According to Wolff, MT has mistakenly read ד for ר and doubled the ' on

is, however, unnecessary, partly because the MT is understandable as it is and partly because the textual correction mars the statement about the election.[76] ידע should here be understood in the same way as מצא and ראה (9.10; see above, pp. 66-67). With R. Bach it can be said that 'the word here indicates the beginning of the special relationship between Yahweh and Israel, that is to say, the 'election'.[77] The repetition of ידע from v. 4b, which Wolff sees as an argument for an incorrect reading, should on the contrary be regarded as a conscious pun on precisely this word. The people of Israel know their God—he has known them and has therefore chosen them. A corresponding formulation of this close relationship between God and his people is also evident in the so-called covenant formula: I will walk among you, and *I will be your God*, and *you shall be my people* (Lev. 26.12).[78] The relationship between God and his people is understood to be reciprocal, and the use of ידע with all of its theological connotations is not due to a 'reading out' (*Verlesung*) but to a carefully thought out formulation. ידע is the 'catchword' in the pericope 13.4-8, regardless of whether it is an original unit[79] or possibly redactionally put together from vv. 4 and 5-8.

That this is the case is supported by the concluding verb in the accusing portion of the unit: שכחוני, they forgot me (v. 6b). According to Wolff[80] there is a close conceptual connection between ידע and שכח. While *knowing God* indicates the religious 'duty', *forgetting God* is the designation of original sin.[81] The metaphorical section of Yahweh's accusation against Israel is thus surrounded by clear speech: they should

the basis of the preceding אני, all under the influence of v. 4b; Wolff, *Hosea*, p. 220; thus also among others Sellin, *Das Zwölfprophetenbuch*, pp. 100-101; Rudolph, *Hosea*, p. 238; Kümpel, *Die Berufung Israels*, pp. 82-83.

76.   Other reasons are mentioned by Bach, 'Erwählung', pp. 36-37; Neef, *Heilstraditionen*, pp. 102-103.

77.   Bach, 'Erwählung', p. 37.

78.   Hos. 2.25b, which is most often considered to be a later insertion, also plays upon the covenant formula. We also find the self-introduction formula in Lev. 26.12ff.

79.   Wolff, *Hosea*, p. 223; Rudolph, *Hosea*, pp. 240ff.; Mays, *Hosea*, p. 174; *et al.*

80.   'Wissen um Gott', pp. 188-93.

81.   This is Wolff's conclusion after an investigation of Hos. 13.4-8; 2.15; 4.6; 8.14. With this in mind, Wolff's emendation in 13.5a comes as an even greater surprise.

know no other gods than Yahweh, but they have forgotten him (vv. 4 and 6b). The metaphor in vv. 5-6a makes the same claim.

Yahweh got to know his flock when they grazed in the wilderness like the flocks of the nomads. And not in just a cognitive sense. ידע designates—as we have seen previously—the election, that is, that Yahweh took responsibility for the flock and took care of their grazing. But the abundance of the grass caused the flock to forget the shepherd because of the grass. Corresponding accusations are put forward many times in the book of Hosea, most strongly in 2.9-10; 10.1. The metaphorical section describes the problem more clearly, namely, that it is a question of a defection to other gods. This is also obviously the case here, although v. 6a also contains an accusation for believing that the grass does not come from anyone in particular, but that the people can perfectly well take care of themselves. The factual section and the metaphorical section illuminate and complement each another; hubris and the belief in self-sufficiency are the cause of forgetfulness, the lack of faith in the one true God.

The threat of punishment in vv. 7-8[82] continues to employ the same metaphor. Yahweh will punish his flock in the figure of the wild animals, which watch for an opportunity while they are grazing.[83] The change of tense, where v. 7a begins with a so-called *tempus historicum*, whereafter vv. 7b-8 switch over to imperfects, means, with the words of Rudolph, that 'this horrible change in the relationship to Yahweh has already been experienced, but it will also be experienced again in the future'.[84] The punishment came upon them already in the wilderness.

The Tradition
How does this stand up to the common perception that we have encountered previously and will meet again in section D, according to which Hosea understands the apostasy as related to the settlement of the cultivated land? The question does not appear to have been discussed. Wolff believes that Yahweh led the flock into the cultivated land, where they became satiated, and Rudolph takes v. 6 as an expression of 'his care...(that) also continued after the period in the wilderness'.[85]

82. Rudolph, *Hosea*, pp. 243-44 *versus* Wolff, *Hosea*, p. 223.
83. Of these the angry mother bear is the worst, according to Rudolph, *Hosea*, p. 243, and what is more, she is to be understood 'proverbially'.
84. Rudolph, *Hosea*, p. 243.
85. Wolff, *Hosea*, p. 226; Rudolph, *Hosea*, p. 243; cf. also Mays, *Hosea*,

But is not this understanding an expression of scholarly conventionalism? The question is raised by the fact that the punishment is said to strike the people already during the period in the wilderness. The punishment must however presuppose that the people have sinned against Yahweh, that they have deserted him. It is true that the Hosean tradition nowhere else deals with an act of apostasy in the wilderness, but this does not mean that it *cannot* do so. If the text is taken as it stands, then there is no place in the pericope where the cultivated land is mentioned. It is true that a grazing in the wilderness that satisfies in abundance is an unusual image, but such images are indeed characteristic of the book of Hosea, which employs rather creative metaphors (see, for example, 9.10-17). There is, therefore, no formal reason for 'rationalizing' the image.

Yahweh's care for his people already during the period of the wandering in the wilderness comes to expression in the fact that the flock grazes and is satiated in the wilderness. At the same time, this image is a good indication of Yahweh's power. We know these traditions from Exodus and Deuteronomy, bus Hosea is also familiar with this idea. It turned up in 12.14, where a prophet (Moses?) is the shepherd on Yahweh's behalf.

The people's apostasy during the wilderness period is set forth in the stories about the people's 'murmuring' in the wilderness. Bach believes that the finding tradition in the book of Hosea and elsewhere is a conscious contradiction of the people's 'murmuring'.[86] Bach's understanding will be dealt with critically in Chapter 5. The analyses in this chapter support his understanding that a finding tradition existed, or in any case a metaphor of the finding, but 13.4-8 would seem to call for a more nuanced view of the use of the image than Bach's. Bach sees a clear contradiction between the finding tradition and the tradition of the people's disobedience in the wilderness. The text itself contradicts him: in accord with their pasture[87] they became satisfied and forgot Yahweh. It was his election that made the grazing so satisfying, but they forgot that. They were therefore already punished during the wilderness period.

In the pericope 13.4-8 we find yet another image that is used to set forward Hosea's accusation against the people that they are living

---

p. 175; Neef, *Heilstraditionen*, p. 103; Bach, 'Erwählung', p. 37.
    86.   Bach, 'Erwählung', p. 1. The finding tradition is also located by Bach in Jeremiah, in Ezekiel, and in Deut. 32; see further below Chapter 5.
    87.   Wolff, *Hosea*, p. 220.

contrary to Yahweh's demand to them concerning דעת אלהים. The finding tradition is worked out here differently from what is generally the case, but the accusation is the same, and the punishment is just as hard as that which came to expression in Hosea 9.[88]

D. The Call in the Cultivated Land

Hosea 10.11-13a: Context
The pericope about *the threshing heifer*, 10.11-13a, is an independent rhetorical unit, which is now part of a larger transmitted unit, 10.9-15, of which the theme is מלחמה, war.[89] The pericope consists of three oracles, 10.9-10, 11-13a, 13b-15, which all have the same point of departure, namely, events in the past, either the distant or the most recent past. The first and the final oracles are similar in regard to both form and content:

9a	The sin in Gibeah and now	13b	The sins of the past
9b	War is on the way	14a	War has started
10a	The kind of war	14b	The kind of war
10b	The cause of war	15	The cause of war and its result

Verses 13b-15 sharpen and specify what has been threatened in vv. 9-10, namely מלחמה, the word that semantically binds the two oracles together.[90] The war is the result of past and ongoing sins. Verses 9-10 have their point of departure in an event that occurred long ago, but which event cannot be known.[91] Also uncertain is what is meant by the

---

88. It is usually stated that the way of thinking in Hos. 13.4-8 is continued directly in Deut. 6; 8 (thus, for example, Wolff, *Hosea*, p. 226). There it is warned that the *coming* satisfaction in the *cultivated* land will cause the people to forget Yahweh. This warning does not, however, disprove that Hosea can speak about a satisfaction in the wilderness in the same way as Exodus does, even if Hosea is recognized as 'one of the fathers of the early Deuteronomic movement' (Wolff, *ibid.*).

89. Wolff, *Hosea*, p. 182.

90. This is the only pericope in the book of Hosea where the word מלחמה is employed (Wolff, *Hosea*, p. 182).

91. It is unlikely that the sin at Gibeah refers to the institution of Saul's monarchy, 1 Sam. 10; see among others Wolff, *Hosea*, pp. 163 and 184; Rudolph, *Hosea*, pp. 179-80 and p. 199. Rudolph believes that the events in Judg. 19–21 are being referred to, but this can in principle be neither proved nor dismissed. The fact that Rudolph, *Hosea*, pp. 199-200, regards it as necessary to emend the text in order to make it fit the events, undermines his idea. In addition, Judg. 19–21 have the character of literary writing rather than historical report. With regard to these

reference ot Gibeah's double sin (v. 10)[92] and by the events that are described in v. 14;[93] but this verse clearly plays upon the idea that Shalmanezer's destruction of Beth-arbel still lives on in the minds of the people. A more precise determination of the events referred to in the two oracles does not play a decisive role for understanding the theology in question. The prophet's intention is clear enough: 'You began to sin already in the distant past, and you are still sinning. Therefore, war will come (which you already are familiar with; v. 14b) as Yahweh's punishment, and (adds v. 15b) the king will be eradicated', that is to say, the final political destruction of Israel will occur.

In the two oracles Hosea takes his point of departure in the relatively recent past, namely, the period in the cultivated land. It is not a question here of some kind of 'golden age', where the relationship between Yahweh and Israel was in order. Israel's stay in the cultivated land has been marked by sin from the very beginning (cf. 2.17; 9.10). That is why the punishment now takes place, namely, the war that destroys everything.

Text

The oracle about the threshing heifer, Hos. 10.11-13a, has been inserted—redactionally[94]—into this easily understood message. The placement of the oracle, which in itself does not deal with war, is explained by the fact that it illustrates the kind of sin that called down Yahweh's punishment.[95] It must be understood as a statement about election and apostasy. But is it an election before or after the settlement in the cultivated land? Is it possible to identify (as some of the commentaries do) the election in 10.11 with the election in the wilderness? Is the threshing heifer that is made into a hardworking draught animal only—as the grapes in the wilderness, 9.10—a surprising picture of the (as yet) innocent—and clever—Israel?

reservations, Rudolph's use of Hos. 9.9 to answer the question about the age of Judg. 19–21 (*Hosea*, p. 180) is not convincing.

92.   Read Q; cf. *BHSd*.

93.   Wolff, *Hosea*, pp. 187-88.

94.   There is no reason to regard the oracle, or portions of it (Marti, *Das Dodekapropheton*, p. 84; Nowack, *Die kleinen Propheten*, p. 64; Vollmer, *Geschichtliche Rückblicke*, pp. 72-73) as secondary (cf. Wolff, *Hosea*, p. 185; Neef, *Heilstraditionen*, p. 84).

95.   עולה (10.13, 9; cf. *BHSd*) can be understood as a catch word (Mays, *Hosea*, p. 145).

11 ואפרים עגלה מלמדה אהבתי לדוש
   ואני עברתי על־טוב צוארה
   ארכיב אפרים יחרוש יהודה ישדד־לו יעקב
12 זרעו לכם לצדקה קצרו לפי־חסד
   נירו לכם ניר ועת לדרוש את־יהוה
   עד־יבוא וירה צדק לכם
13 חרשתם־רשע עולתה קצרתם
   אכלתם פרי־כחש

11 Ephraim was a trained heifer,
   who loved to thresh.
   I came along and saw his fair neck.
   I harnessed Ephraim,
   Judah plowed
   Jacob harrowed.
12 'You will sow in righteousness
   You will harvest in faithfulness.
   You will break up fallow ground.
   The time has come to seek Yahweh,
   so that he will come
   and let justice flow down'.
13 You have plowed in unrighteousness
   and harvested evil
   and eaten the fruits of lies.

A couple of remarks are necessary with regard to the translation.[96] Rudolph lists three possible understandings of the verb עבר, v. 11a: (1) 'to pass by sparingly' (cf. Mic. 7.18; Prov. 19.11); (2) 'to come by, (by chance) pass by' (cf. Ezek. 16.6, 8);[97] (3) 'to fall upon (with hostile intent)' (cf. Nah. 3.19; Job 9.11).[98] In spite of Rudolph's objections, to which I will shortly return, the second suggestion, 'I came by', is the most appropriate, especially in light of Gen. 18.5.[99] If we moreover assume that Bach's perception of the syntax in v. 11a is correct,[100] namely, that it is a circumstantial clause that more precisely dates the preceding nominal

---

96. For text-critical considerations, see Wolff, *Hosea*, pp. 179-80.
97. A parallel is found in Hos. 9.10, מצא; see also Gen. 18.5; 1 Kgs 9.8; 2 Kgs 4.9.
98. Rudolph himself emends, in that he cannot accept any of the suggestions: עברתי → על עברתי (pi'el instead of hif. according to special Northern Israelite linguistic usage; cf. the suggestion העברתי, *BHSa*); על has fallen out due to haplography (*Hosea*, pp. 201-202).
99. Cf. also Wolff, *Hosea*, p. 179.
100. 'Erwählung', pp. 20-21.

clause, then the half-verse stands forth as the specification of a condition that has been changed by Yahweh's intervention. We have before us the picture of the threshing heifer, who is 'discovered' by a passer-by.

In v. 11b the strange use of *Judah* has led to different explanations, of which the best is that an original *Israel* has been changed to *Judah* in connection with a Judaean redaction.[101] Wolff retains the MT while noting that 'Judah' is perfectly understandable in the context of the settlement of the land;[102] there is, however, no real need to regard the oracle as a reference to the traditions of the settlement (see below, pp. 88-90), and the tight structure, where three statements constantly say the same thing, indicates that there were originally three synonymous designations for the Northern Kingdom, namely, Ephraim, Israel and Jacob.[103]

Wolff suggests that there be read דעת instead of רעת with LXX and Targ.[104] Versus Wolff, it must be maintained that the picture in v. 12a of Yahweh's צדק as a rain that provides fertility cannot be removed from the context without a significant loss of meaning (see below). The suggestion of a correction is due to conventionalism, and Wolff's suggestion for the changes to be made in v. 12 is on the whole based upon a somewhat mechanical (protestant?) understanding of Hosea's theology.[105] Rudolph's suggested correction of v. 13b, insertion of the copula ו before אלהים, must also be rejected.[106] The form-critical considerations—that the oracle must conclude with a threat of punishment and that the chiasm in v. 13a indicates such a change—are not convincing. The

---

101.   Emmerson, *Hosea*, pp. 85-86. We have previously observed this 'modernizing form' in Hos. 12.3.

102.   *Hosea*, p. 179.

103.   The original oracle was therefore probably as follows:

   I harnessed Ephraim,
   Israel plowed,
   Jacob harrowed.

But with this a textual correction is, of course, not being suggested.

104.   Wolff, *Hosea*, p. 180. Wolff's suggestion is a perfectly reasonable reading, in that צדקה, חסד and דעת belong within the same semantic field (see 2.21-22; 4.1; 6.6); but the text must be preserved as a *lectio difficilior* and makes good sense, in that the righteousness, which according to v. 12b will flow down like rain (ירה II), will come upon the newly broken, virgin, and unperverted ground. The suggested correction of ירה → פרי in v. 12b (KB, *s.v.* ירה; Wolff, *ibid.*) is unnecessary.

105.   Compare also Rudolph's remarks in *Hosea*, p. 201.

106.   Rudolph, *Hosea*, pp. 201-204.

oracle concludes powerfully with the open statement about Israel's offence. It could possibly be that a later redactor's perception that a direct threat was missing contributed to the present placement of the oracle. But this possibility remains pure speculation.

Metaphor

Hos. 10.11-13a is, therefore, an oracle about the disobedience of the chosen people. But which election is in question? According to J. Jeremias, עבר על is to be understood as a *terminus technicus* for Yahweh's theophany on Sinai—especially in the Northern Kingdom.[107] It is normally claimed that Hosea is speaking about events that took place during the period in the wilderness when he employs the image of the threshing heifer.[108] If, however, material from the history of religions is taken into consideration, which has particularly been true of Scandinavian research, then the possibility of another understanding emerges.

Excursus 1
The Cult of Yahweh and the Canaanite Fertility Cult

We shall therefore briefly leave Hosea 10 and for a moment direct our attention to a discussion of *the fertility cult* and its terminological influence on the forms of expression in the book of Hosea. There is a long tradition for making comparisons between the book of Hosea and the Ugaritic texts. F. Hvidberg's pioneer work, *Graad og Latter i Det gamle Testamente* from 1938,[109] is well known. One of the more recent studies in this tradition is D. Kinet's *Ba'al und Jahwe* from 1977. Kinet here attempts a motif-oriented reading of the Ugaritic texts' picture of Baal and a parallel reading of the picture of Yahweh in the book of Hosea, after which the book's third part is a Summary Comparison (*Zusammenfassender Vergleich*) of the two gods.

In his introduction to this final section, Kinet calls attention to the fundamental problems that are involved in such a comparison. Two different types of religion cannot be meaningfully analyzed by asking the same questions. The problems that thereby arise, however, can at the same time elucidate where there are possibilities for comparison and where there are not. A greater difficulty for Kinet's enterprise is that the Canaanite religiosity that Hosea is up against is not *identical* with that found in the

---

107. Jeremias, *Hosea*, p. 134.
108. Wolff, *Hosea*, p. 185; Rudolph, *Hosea*, p. 203; Jeremias, *Hosea*, pp. 134-35; Bach, 'Erwählung', p. 21. Cf. also Mays, *Hosea*, p. 145: 'The heifer (Ephraim) already belongs to the man (Yahweh)...'
109. ET 1962: *Weeping and Laughter in the Old Testament*.

Ugaritic texts. The religion of the Ugaritic texts probably reflects an official (court?) religion, a learned Baal theology, while what Hosea fought against is popular religion, a practical—and practised—Baal piety.[110] In this regard it must not be forgotten that Baal had many different, local manifestations—every town (or family) had its Baal.

There are in addition two further problems, namely, first of all, the geographical and chronological distance between Ugarit and the Northern Kingdom at the time of Hosea,[111] and second, that the picture we have of Israelite religiosity in the book of Hosea is strongly polemical. These problems do not mean, however, that the picture of Canaanite religion that has been shaped on the basis of the Ugaritic texts cannot shed light upon the book of Hosea—and perhaps to a greater degree than Kinet dares to claim. N.P. Lemche would appear to be right when he perceives features in the Ugaritic material that point forward to religious features in Israel in the first millennium BCE as 'indications of the basis upon which Israelite religion evolved'.[112] It is in fact no longer possible as a matter of course to maintain a sharp dichotomy between Israel and Canaan. On the basis of the sociological research made of Israel's earliest period, the relevance of considering the Canaanites as a different people (*ethnos*) from the Israelites is now questioned.[113] If the Israelites were in fact from an ethnic point of view Canaanites, then it will also be possible to understand the Israelite folk religion as Canaanite. The word *Canaanite* (which moreover is not used in the book of Hosea) becomes thereby a designation for the popular—not Yahweh-monistic—religion,[114] which is opposed *in casu* by Hosea and his followers—it is not a designation of a foreign religion.[115]

Hosea 5.8-6.6 provides a clear exposition of the relationship between prophetic theology and the popular theology of fertility. The pericope is usually understood on the basis of A. Alt's epoch making article[116] to be dealing with the Syro-Ephraimite war and its theological implications, as Hosea has seen them. It is in any case certain that these verses are concerned with an emergency situation, in which Ephraim first seeks help from Assyria, the vassal Lord (5.13), but without success, because it is Yahweh who is the cause of the emergency. He has wounded them, and he will withdraw from them until they repent and seek him (5.14). In 6.1-3 follows Ephraim's[117] song of repentance and in 6.4-6 Yahweh's response of rejection. The pericope is composed of several oracles, which are, however, semantically related. They may well

110.   *Ba'al und Jahwe*, pp. 209-10; cf. below Chapter 4, Section B.

111.   *Ba'al und Jahwe*, pp. 8-9.

112.   Lemche, *Ancient Israel*, p. 199; cf. also E. Hammershaimb, *Some Aspects of Old Testament Prophecy from Isaiah to Malachi*, p. 68 n. 13.

113.   Thus, for example, N.K. Gottwald, *The Tribes of Yahweh*; G.W. Ahlström, *Who were the Israelites?*; Lemche, *Early Israel*, and especially *idem, The Canaanites and their Land*.

114.   See further in this regard Chapter 4, Section B.

115.   The word 'Canaanite' should therefore properly be put in quotation marks in order to indicate that it is being used in a different fashion than was the case in previous literature.

116.   'Hosea 5,8–6,6. Ein Krieg und seine Folgen in Prophetischer Beleuchtung'. Otherwise Good, 'Hosea 5,8–6,6: An Alternative to Alt', who understands Hos. 5.8–6.6 as part of a cultic event, in which a covenant lawsuit is included.

117.   And Judah's. 'Judah' in 5.10-14 is original, and not a later Judaean gloss, Emmerson, *Hosea*, pp. 68ff.

constitute an original unit, but it is also possible that there are several originally independent oracles that have been secondarily woven together, because they move within the same thematic and metaphorical universe.[118] The semantic-thematic relationship comes most clearly to view in 5.11-14, 15 and 6.1-3; and even though the two pericopes can and ought to be differentiated form-critically, it is not possible to do so with regard to content. It is not necessary to discuss the authenticity of the individual members; nothing indicates the presence of secondary accretions, and 6.4-6 also belongs quite naturally to the context. There is, therefore, much to indicate that in 5.11–6.6 (or 5.8–6.6) we find a unit that comes from the early Hosean tradition. But the genesis of the pericope cannot finally be determined.

Hos. 6.1-3 occupies a central place in the pericope. It is not an authentic popular penitential song,[119] but a penitential song composed by Hosea (or the early Hosean circle) and put into the mouth of repentant Israel.[120] It is thus pointless to discuss whether the people really and honestly believe what they say or whether they are trying to cheat Yahweh and are therefore rejected. The semantic examples that show that 6.1-3 belongs to the earliest layers of the Hosean tradition—the affinities between this section and that preceding—have already been set forth by Alt.[121] In this regard the significant use of ידע in 6.3a should be noted. As we have seen previously, it is in connection with דעת אלהים an expression of Hosea's conception of theology. When the people in v. 3aα are quoted as saying they will strive to know Yahweh: ונדעה נרדפה לדעת את־יהוה, Hosea is saying with other words that they think they are doing what he wishes. But the context clearly shows that they do not do it.[122]

118. Cf. for example, Hentschke, *Die Stellung der vorexilischen Schriftpropheten zum Kultus*, pp. 89; Mays, *Hosea*, p. 87.

119. The origin and *Sitz im Leben* of Hos. 6.1-3 is a matter of scholarly debate: May suggests that it may originate in a Baal liturgy, 'The Fertility Cult in Hosea', others that it is a penitential song sung by the priests or the people on a day of repentance (cf., for example, Wolff, *Hosea*, pp. 117-19; Hentschke, *Die Stellung*, p. 89; Rudolph, *Hosea*, p. 130), others that it is an answer to Hosea's preaching, cf. Mays, *Hosea*, p. 94. Interpretations of Hos. 6.1-3 are legion: Humbert calls the passage a light-hearted hymn (*Leichtsinnspsalm*, see Sellin, *Das Zwölfprophetenbuch*, p. 71); Wellhausen and many others after him speak about the 'false hope' of the people (*Die kleinen Propheten*, p. 116); Sellin believes that Yahweh 'clearly demands something incomparably more serious and deeper' (*Das Zwölfprophetenbuch*, p. 70); along the same lines are Alt, 'Hosea 5,8–6,6', pp. 184-85; Wolff, *Dodekapropheton*, I, p. 149; Kinet, *Ba'al und Jahwe*, p. 155 with n. 16. With regard to these understandings, Hvidberg may ask 'what the prophet, after all, may demand more than the conversion to Yahweh and recognition of Yahweh expressed in Verses 1 and 3...' (*Weeping and Laughter*, p. 127); and H. Schmidt, 'Hosea 6.1-6', p. 123, speaks of the people's 'genuine seriousness' and 'heartfelt trust'; see also (from more recent research) Rudolph, *Hosea*, p. 134; Hentschke, *Die Stellung*, p. 91.

120. Hvidberg, *Weeping and Laughter*, p. 126. An interesting interpretation is set forth by Alt, who believes that Hosea had received 5.12-14 before 5.15–6.6, but in order to make himself understood he had to repeat the earlier oracle before he reproduced the one he had received later on ('Hosea 5,8-6,6', pp. 183-84).

121. טרף 6.1 = 5.14 (both times in relation to Yahweh) רפא 6.1 = 5.13 (transposed from the Great King to Yahweh), the placing next to each other of Ephraim and Judah 6.4 = 5.12-14 (with the omission of ב), ('Hosea 5,8-6,6', p. 183 with n. 2).

122. Versus Rudolph, *Hosea*, p. 134.

This is to be seen not only from the fact that the penitential song is rejected, but also because of the semantic dependence of the song upon the Canaanite fertility cult. Most commentators are in agreement on this matter,[123] but there is not agreement as to the degree and significance of this dependence. There is no reason to deny that there lies a fertility cult *phenomenology* behind the expression in 6.1-3 and that the book of Hosea makes use of a cultic form, the penitential psalm, but in inverted form. First of all, it is shown that repentance is made impossible by an incorrect theology. Secondly, according to 6.4-6 the prophet does not announce Yahweh's forgiveness and a promise of assistance, which is what the penitent would expect, but on the contrary a rejection of assistance and a renewed threat of punishment together with a declaration concerning what Yahweh really wishes.[124] Popular theology comes first and foremost to expression in the conceptions that lie behind v. 2:

יחינו מימים ביום השלישי יקמני

After two days he will revive us,
on the third day he will raise us up.

The conception of the resurrection of the dead has its place in the fertility cult, and scholars have often attempted to find the idea concerning the two day's stay in the kingdom of the dead and the resurrection on the third day in the ancient Near Eastern parallel material.[125] Thus Hvidberg believes that 'the expression "after two days" in parallel with "on the third day" looks like a formula, which has not been conceived by the prophet, but which he took over'. Hvidberg does not succeed, however, in finding any parallels in the Ras Shamra materials.[126] In spite of his reservations,

---

123. But see Rudolph, *Hosea*, p. 136.

124. Another example of such an inverted use of a cultic form is found in Jer. 14, the great drought-lament, where Yahweh also in v. 10 refuses to help the penitent. Cf. Mowinckel, *Zur Komposition des Buches Jeremia*, pp. 22-23; *idem, Offersang og sangoffer*, pp. 194-220; I have dealt with this liturgy in *Fra profeti til prædiken*, pp. 437-46, especially pp. 442-43. The connection is also mentioned by H. Schmidt, 'Hosea 6,1-6', p. 121, who in fact takes his point of departure in among other passages Jer. 14 in order to determine that Hos. 6.1-6 is a 'song for a day of repentance' (*Busstagsgesang*); see in addition Hvidberg, *Weeping and Laughter*, pp. 126-27; Good, 'Hosea 5,8–6,6', pp. 284ff. Incidentally, Jer. 14.10b is a quotation of Hos. 8.13, presumably used by Jeremiah himself. See in this regard *Fra profeti til prædiken*, p. 443 with n. 4; cf. W. Thiel, *Die deuteronomistische Redaktion von Jeremia 1–25*, p. 181. We also find dependence upon Hosean thought and vocabulary in the second lament psalm in Jer. 14 (vv. 17-22).

125. Some scholars (especially German speaking) reject the notion that there is a conception of the resurrection of the dead in Hos. 6.2, which is often understood as an expression for healing. See, for example, Rudolph, *Hosea*, pp. 136-37; Wolff, *Hosea*, pp. 118-19; Kinet, *Ba'al und Jahwe*, pp. 155-56 with n. 10. Correspondingly then the two or three days in the kingdom of the dead are regarded as a proverbial specification of the short duration involved; see, for example, Rudolph, *Hosea*, p. 137.

126. Hvidberg, *Weeping and Laughter*, pp. 128ff. At an early point in modern scholarship, W.W. Baudissin, *Adonis und Esmun*, pp. 403-16, goes further, in that he finds parallels with Adonis. A similar argument is set forth by K. Jeppesen (who tentatively wants to see a connection between, on the one hand, the Sumerian myth about the goddess Inanna's descent into the kingdom of the dead, where a resurrection on the third day is hinted at, and, on the other hand, the suffering people

Kinet's understanding is, therefore, the most probable one:

> The torn apart and beaten people reminds one first and foremost of the fate of Baal...the Baal myth has however in no way been appropriated in a rigorous fashion.[127]

It is simply a question of the death of a god and his resurrection, which is a phenomenon known from the entire geographical region (and in relation to the Old Testament from Ugarit),[128] but there is no question of a specific version of this myth. This is to be seen precisely in the announcement of the two- to three-day period, which does not characterize a particular god's resurrection, but is best understood as an expression of the conviction that the resurrection will occur.[129]

Verse 3aβ comes closer to expressing a particular theology, where Yahweh's coming is compared with שחר, dawn, one of the two so-called 'beaux dieux' in Ugaritic mythology.[130] The mythical features become even clearer in the continuation: Yahweh is said to come like the rain, like the life-giving spring rain that waters (ירה II) the earth. The text does *not* say that he *sends* this rain; it compares—without directly identifying—Yahweh with dawn and rain. Hosea is making sarcastic remarks about the people's apparent piety by using terms from popular religion. He there finds a mixing of Yahweh terminology (ידע)[131] and the fertility cult, which the people apparently believe is the proper Yahweh faith (cf. Hos. 2.8-15): 'Let us return to Yahweh', he has them say, not from another cult, but from the failed

---

as Yahweh's wife), who says that they will rise from the dead (K. Jeppesen, 'Myth in the Prophetic Literature', p. 105 n. 25; Jeppesen refers to F. Stolz, *Strukturen und Figuren im Kult von Jerusalem*).

127. Kinet, *Ba'al und Jahwe*, p. 156.

128. See in this regard the texts I*AB; I AB, *ANET²*, pp. 138-41; cf. also A. Caquot, *Textes Ougaritiques*, I, pp. 225-71 (including the bibliography, pp. 237-38).

129. With regard to the time interval between the different gods' death and resurrection, see Hvidberg, *Weeping and Laughter*, pp. 128ff. Hvidberg is perhaps correct in his supposition: 'Perhaps a closer examination of the total material in the Old Testament concerning 'the third day' might suggest that the 'two days' (time of damnation, death) and the 'third day' (day of crisis, beginning of the time of blessing) were an ancient mythical motif in the Orient, it must be supposed to have arisen' (*Weeping and Laughter*, p. 129). Another and more prosaic explanation of the number sequence two–three is found by W.M.W. Roth, 'The Numerical Sequence x/x+1 in the Old Testament', who sees such a number sequence (x/x + 1) as 'a stylistic device of common usage in both prose and poetry' (p. 311). This stylistic device is widespread in both the Old Testament and other ancient Near Eastern literature. It is a constituent part of *parallelismus membrorum*, but is in no way limited to the numbers two and three (examples in Roth).

130. See in this regard the text 'SS (La Naissance des Dieux)' with introduction and bibliography, Caquot, *Textes Ougaritiques*, I, pp. 359-79. The text is moreover highly controversial.

131. In an extension of an interpretation of the verb ידע in a sexual context, i.e., on the basis of Hos. 1–3, it could legitimately be considered as to whether the fertility aspect is also present here; compare also Jeppesen's considerations (see above, p. 84 n. 126). I do not believe, however, that this is the case. The verb רדף with Israel as the subject is also used pejoratively in 2.9; 12.2 (see Jeremias, *Hosea*, p. 86).

belief in political solutions. The song of penitence in Hos. 6.1-3 describes conceptions from a 'canaanite' Yahweh faith, where the people seek Yahweh as a nature
god.[132] It reproduces their words, but with the prophetic intention in mind: bitter
contempt for their foolishness. The irony is deadly and the song of penitence, 6.1-3, is followed by a total rejection
in vv. 4-6. Yahweh rejects—after an almost paternal lament in v. 4a—the חסד they
have shown, that is, the faithfulness to the one true God, whom they have claimed they
want to know. Their faithfulness is inconstant like the morning cloud.[133] Yahweh will
come—not to re-establish, but to judge.[134] Faithfulness to and knowledge of God are
what is required, not the sacrificial cult.[135]

In the pericope 5.8–6.6 there is yet an expression that has an affinity with 10.12,
namely 5.15aβb:

עד אשר־יאשמו ובקשו פני
בצר להם ישחרנני

until they acknowledge their guilt and seek my face.
In their distress they will earnestly seek me.

Is there any connection between the two passages—and is there perhaps a connection
with the Canaanite conception of the goddess, who looks for her dead lover? First of
all, it must be noted that different verbs are employed in 5.15 and 10.12, namely בקש
(pi'el) and שחר (pi'el) in 5.15; דרש in 10.12. שחר is presumably found here in its
earliest context;[136] its synonymy with בקש is evident from both the form of the verse
and an investigation of its other—not especially numerous—appearances in the Old
Testament (qal 1×, pi'el 13×).

According to Westermann,[137] בקש has as its basic meaning 'to look for something
that has been lost', something that one once possessed. In the sense of 'to seek God'
the verb occurs with two variations in meaning, one where it is a question of an
isolated act (among these Hos. 5.6), and the other where the content of meaning has
been generalized to mean 'abide by God', thus more a *status* than an *actus*. In the last
sense (which also covers Hos. 5.15) the verb becomes synonymous with דרש in later
occurrences. At the same time, Westermann rejects the idea that in the context of 'to

---

132.   Cf. Hentschke, *Die Stellung*, p. 91.
133.   Note how Hosea again plays upon natural phenomena. This is resumed in v. 5b: 'my
judgment goes forth as the light' (*BHS e-e*).
134.   See Good, 'Hosea 5,8–6,6', pp. 280-81.
135.   Cf. Hentschke, *Die Stellung*, pp. 88-89. See also 5.6, which says that Yahweh does not
let himself be pacified by sacrifices. See in this regard Hentschke, *Die Stellung*, pp. 91-93.
136.   The root שחר is found again as a substantive in 6.3. There is an etymological connection
between the two words (see GKB, *s.v.* שחר II), and the verb has presumably been chosen precisely to
create a connection between the two verses, but there does not appear to be any spill-over with
regard to the meaning. The key-word technique is frequently used in the book of Hosea, see, for
example, עון Hos. 12.
137.   'Die Begriffe für Fragen und Suchen im Alten Testament'.

seek God' there is a search in any real sense of the word. On the contrary. One cannot seek—and find—God, as the bride does her lover in Song of Songs 3. God's remoteness is overcome by God alone, when he answers the abandoned person's prayer.[138] Yahweh is only to be found when he *will* let himself be found.[139]

It is clear, however, that he whom they have lost because he has withdrawn himself from them *can* be found when the one who seeks has repented. The basic meaning of בקש, which Westermann stresses, namely to seek what one has lost, resounds also in דרש. People can find God. The text, however, does not resound with the mythology of the goddess seeking the dead god, the seeking that the people in the Canaanite cult also have participated in, in any case in Ugarit[140] (and in Mesopotamia). There is an important difference between Anat's seeking for the murdered Baal and the people's seeking for the God who has withdrawn himself and who is able to return by his own power. בקש, שחר and דרש in the book of Hosea describe seeking God there where he must be assumed to be, namely at the sanctuary. If they come with the proper attitude, then he will meet them (10.12; 5.15). If they look for him with sacrifices that are supposed to 'force' him to come forward, then they will not find him (5.6-7).

Hosea's conceptions about seeking Yahweh are often compared with Amos 5.5-6, where the people are warned against seeking Yahweh at the sanctuaries in Bethel, Gilgal and Beersheba: one seeks Yahweh by hearing his word through the prophet. Hosea 12 is also understood in this fashion.[141] But can Amos's strong criticism of the cult be transferred to Hosea? It is not unreasonable to presume that behind the interpretation of the phrase 'to seek Yahweh' as corresponding to the words 'to seek his word through the prophets' there is an influence on modern scholarship from Deuteronomistic theology, which indicates among other things the idea of the centralization of the cult and prophetic theology. But this is all far later than Hosea and ought not to have any influence upon our understanding of his theology. Hosea is not hostile to the cult *per se*, but he is critical of the present misuse of the cult, in the same way that his perception that the priests have failed in their task to teach the people דעת אלהים does not lead him to reject the priesthood as such (he himself takes over forms of the priestly functions), but on the contrary to condemn the *present* priests. We have seen in Chapter 2 how he does not unequivocally distance himself

<hr />

138.   If we investigate the use of בקש (pi'el) and דרש in the book of Hosea, it is seen that in 2.9 it is a question of seeking the lovers, i.e., idols. 7.10-11, which has a certain relationship with 5.5-6, states that the people do not seek Yahweh, but political solutions (compare also 5.13). In 5.6 they are seeking, but are not *finding* God, who has withdrawn from them without mercy. 5.15, on the other hand, hints at the possibility that Yahweh will himself be found again, when they repent; and in 10.12 it is promised that he will indeed come, when they seek him. 3.5 is reckoned to be either a later addition (Clements, *Prophecy and Tradition*, p. 30) or a Judaean gloss (see, for example, Wolff, *Hosea*, p. 57. If the latter is the case, then we have a use of בקש that approaches that of דרש.

139.   Yahweh is the object for מצא only in 5.6.

140.   See in this regard Kapelrud, *The Violent Goddess*, pp. 89ff.

141.   See, for example, W.H. Schmidt, 'Suchet den Herrn, so werdet Ihr leben', esp. pp. 127-34.

from the sanctuary in Bethel, and an investigation of other passages, where the sanctuaries in Bethel and Gilgal are chiefly mentioned can lead to corresponding results.[142] There is thus no reason to regard the summons to seek God as anything other than a request to seek him in the right way. That is to say, as described in 6.6 with חסד and דעת אלהים, and at the right place, namely at the sanctuary. This is the simplest and earliest understanding of דרש and also applies to בקש in this context.[143]

With the above reflections in mind we can now return to the use of fertility terminology in Hos. 10.11-13a. In Ugaritic religion the *heifer* is the symbol of the goddess Anat, who, previous to Baal's descent into the kingdom of the dead, enters into a *hieros gamos* with him in the form of a bull.[144] After his death she fights with Mot, the god of the dead, whom she defeats. The struggle is described in a way that reminds one of the processing of the ripe grain.[145] On the basis of the Ugaritic texts, H. Gottlieb believes that a threshing rite is being described, which at the time of the harvest festival illustrates the victory over the powers of chaos. Such a rite is also known from Egyptian materials, and Gottlieb argues for the existence of a correponding Israelite rite. He refers as well to the apparently sacral character of the cities' threshing places.[146]

When viewed against this background, 10.11a provides an extremely charged picture of the relationship between Yahweh and Israel. Israel is portrayed in the figure of Anat with the sexual connotations that are

142. See in this regard Emmerson, *Hosea*, pp. 117-55. She writes with a point of departure in Hos. 4.15: 'The prophet is not concerned to condemn the existence of the sanctuaries at Gilgal and Bethel any more than he is opposed in principle to the oath formula חי־יהוה. He is concerned rather with an apostate nation whose practices defiled ancient and honourable sanctuaries hallowed in Israel's past history as they also dishonoured the oath taken in Yahweh's name. Certainly if the prophet's prohibitions were to be heeded the result would be the cessation of worship at these sanctuaries. Yet it must be recognized that, far from implying hostility on the prophet's part to the sanctuaries concerned, this might rather indicate respect for the honourable past of holy places now defiled by his contemporaries' (p. 126). This last consideration moreover corresponds splendidly with the ideas in Hos. 12.
143. Cf. W.H. Schmidt, 'Suchet den Herrn, so werdet Ihr leben', p. 126.
144. Cf. I*AB (v), *ANET*[2], p. 139.
145. Cf. I AB (ii), *ANET*[2], p. 140. See in this regard Hvidberg, *Weeping and Laughter*, p. 51; H. Gottlieb, 'Den tærskende kvie—Mi 4,11-13', p. 169.
146. 'Den tærskende kvie', pp. 167-71; see further O. Hvidberg-Hansen, 'Die Vernichtung des goldenen Kalbes und der ugaritische Ernteritus. Der rituelle Hintergrund für Exod. 32,20 und andere alttestamentliche Berichte über die Vernichtung von Götterbildern', who identifies a rite in connection with the final growth and the after-grass.

associated with her[147] as well as with the word עגלה, heifer.[148] There is no doubt that Yahweh was worshipped in the figure of the bull or the calf in the Northern Kingdom (cf. Exod. 32; 1 Kgs 12),[149] and the idea that the people have identified Yahweh with Baal is moreover quite obvious in the book of Hosea (6.1-3; 7.13-14; cf. 14.2-4). That Hos. 10.11 should actually be seen as an *interpretatio israëlitica* of the *hieros gamos*, as Gottlieb believes,[150] must certainly be regarded as an exaggeration that is based upon the use of Hosea 1-3 as an interpretative key to the entire book of Hosea. It must be maintained, however, that Hosea is also here using well known material from the Canaanite cult (cf. the metaphors in 2.4-17 and 14.2-9). But he does more than use the material—he contradicts it. The fair heifer is removed from the threshing place (that is, the fertility cult)[151] and placed instead in Yahweh's service. He elects it to service in צדקה and חסד and to prepare the earth, which he will bless with צדק.[152]

In 10.11-13a the election occurs in the cultivated land itself; there is nothing to connect the threshing heifer with the wilderness. On the contrary, the description has a clear connection with an agricultural milieu, both directly and in a cultic sense.[153] The agricultural terminology is

147. Anat is among other things the goddess of love; see, for example, Kapelrud, *The Violent Goddess*, pp. 92-105.

148. Cf. Judg. 14.18; Gottlieb, 'Den tærskende kvie', p. 168.

149. It is interesting to note in this regard Hvidberg-Hansen's interpretation of the destruction of the golden calf as being a reflection on the sacrifice of the final growth, 'Die Vernichtung des goldenen Kalbes und der ugaritische Ernteritus'.

150. 'Den tærskende kvie', p. 168.

151. By way of comparison it can be mentioned how David uses Araunah's threshing sledges for wood and his oxen for burnt offerings (2 Sam. 24.22) and in this way profanes the threshing place as a Jebusite cultic site (see Gottlieb, 'Den tærskende kvie', p. 170). The threshing heifer is also employed in other passages in the Old Testament. Mic. 4.11-13 is well known. In Hos. 4.16 Israel is compared with a rebellious cow, פרע.

152. The shift in metaphor from the draught animal in v. 11 to the farmer in v. 12 does not have any special significance. The controlling metaphor is the same, namely the cultivation of the field. Such a shift is also known, for example, in the courtroom scene in Hos. 2.

153. There is no reason to understand the pericope literally, as Weiser does: 'Hosea compares Ephraim with a cow that is quick to learn, that willingly threshes since it can at the same time eat just as it likes. Apparently Hosea is thinking here of the wilderness period. Then, however, came the period when Israel had to do more difficult work, like the cow, that when it has been harnessed in the yoke, must plow

combined with religious terminology in order to say something about
the relationship between Yahweh and the people, namely, that they are
his possession, which he rules over. The picture shows us that Hosea
does not *exclusively* count on an election in the wilderness. There is,
therefore, no need to read the oracle with the traditions of the settlement
in mind.[154] What Hosea wants to tell is not *when* the people were called,
but *that* they were called to service for Yahweh.

The heifer, that is, the people, is chosen עֵל־טוּב צַוָּארָהּ, *because of its
fair neck*, 10.11aβ. This description of the people's suitability indicates
that Yahweh was not unaware of the people's potential when he chose
them, an interpretation that corresponds well with the election pericope
in Hos. 9.10. טוּב not only designates the heifer's beauty, but also its
usefulness.[155] There is, however, a difference in nuance between the
harmony in 9.10 and the usefulness in 10.11, in that 10.11 does not lay
as much weight on the condition at the time of the election as it does on
future usefulness.[156]

In 10.11-13a, therefore, Hosea does not take his point of departure in
a mythology that we know from the Old Testament, but on the contrary, in a mythology that he opposes. There is no doubt that this
mythology was well-known by many in the prophet's audience, and in
other passages he uses this mythology in the same way, boldly, but
certainly not without effect.

Election ideas are resumed in v. 12, where the emphasis is placed
upon the life that Israel has been chosen for, namely a life that is lived in

and harrow. Apparently the picture and the facts of the matter run into each other here,
so that Hosea appears with the description of this work to designate Israel's activity
as that of a peasant folk in Palestine. This is also to be seen in v. 12, where the picture
of the people is abandoned and where the activity of the peasants themselves is
discussed' (*Hosea*, p. 82).

154. Against Wolff, *Hosea*, p. 185; Jeremias, *Hosea*, p. 135.

155. 'He (Yahweh) observes that this animal with such a neck is capable of more
than simply threshing', writes Wolff, *Hosea*, p. 185.

156. Cf. Jeremias, *Hosea*, pp. 135-36; cf. also Vollmer, *Geschichtliche
Rückblicke*, p. 74. This interpretation is contradicted as already mentioned by
Rudolph, among others, who here as in other places cannot accept any form of merit
on the part of the people. 'If only then (compare 9.10) the interpretation of the picture
does not lead again to the fatal, and for Hosea repugnant, idea that Israel has been
called thanks to its own excellent characteristics!' (Rudolph, *Hosea*, p. 202). But
Rudolph's own interpretation is based on an emendation, which must be regarded as
most unsatisfying.

a proper relationship to God. This life is described in v. 12a with the substantives צדקה/צדק and חסד together with the metaphor נורו לכם ניר.[157]

Excursus 2
The Meaning of צדקה/צדק

צדקה/צדק and חסד[158] are concepts that have their background in social, universally human conditions, but in the book of Hosea they belong semantically to the concept דעת אלהים, knowledge of God, or theology.[159] דעת אלהים contains the demand for an open recognition of Yahweh's historical right to Israel, the demand for exclusivity (see section A);[160] the relationship between Yahweh and Israel is a legal one, of which the priests should inform the people.[161] If the priests succeed in this task—and according to Hos. 4.5-6 they do not—then the people will be able to show חסד before God.

The basic meaning of חסד is, following Zimmerli, best understood as 'proper conduct in a joint relationship',[162] though not in the form of a ceremonial or judicial covenantal agreement, but as a societal moral code.[163] When transferred to the religious sphere, חסד means recognizing through action that Yahweh is the God of the people, but not necessarily in the form of 'covenantal faithfulness', as it is often understood.[164] The idea of a covenantal agreement as theology's centre (*Mitte*) lies, as we have seen in section A, beyond the realm of the book of Hosea.

The concepts צדקה/צדק have, as does the heifer, a religio-historical significance that calls for a closer investigation.[165] According to A. Jepsen, one must distinguish

---

157. This is taken up later by Jeremiah (4.3) and appears, in 'reversed' form, in Prov. 21.4.

158. Concerning חסד see Zimmerli, 'Gottesrecht'; *idem*, 'χάρις'; Jepsen, 'Gnade und Barmherzigkeit im Alten Testament'; concerning צדקה/צדק see Jepsen, 'צדק und צדקה im Alten Testament'; Schmid, *Gerechtigkeit als Weltordnung*. For the connection between the concepts mentioned and דעת אלהים, see Holt, 'דעת אלהים und חסד im Buche Hosea'.

159. This is also the case even if one does not go along with Wolff's correction to דעת ניר, Hos. 10.12a ('Wissen um Gott', p. 183 n. 2; cf. also *Hosea*, p. 180 and p. 185-86). Cf. further Baumann, '"Wissen um Gott" bei Hosea als Urform von Theologie?', pp. 416-25, and Section A above.

160. 'ידע' means mainly, therefore, in Hosea's thinking, an absolutely *one-sided, human* occurrence, in which the human being recalls the past, or, better: in which he or she *knows past events, which can also be forgotten, as presently valid and effective*' (Wolff, 'Wissen um Gott', p. 192, Wolff's emphasis).

161. 'The דעת is (...) in Hosea's view the real and decisive priestly function, or, better yet: the fundamental content of the priestly office' (Wolff, 'Wissen um Gott', p. 187).

162. '...das rechte Verhalten in einer Gemeinschaftsbeziehung' (Zimmerli, 'Gottesrecht', pp. 222-23). The background for this definition is to be found in his article, 'χάρις'. Zimmerli here discusses Glueck's understanding of חסד as a legal obligation as well as Stoebe's contrary understanding, in which חסד is a free act of love.

163. *Cf.* Jepsen, 'Gnade und Barmherzigkeit im Alten Testament', pp. 265ff.

164. Thus also Zimmerli.

165. See K. Koch, 'Sdq im Alten Testament'; *idem*, 'צדק, *sdq*'; Jepsen, 'צדק und צדקה';

between the concepts צדק and צדקה, in that צדק indicates the concept of order *per se*, while צדקה indicates the action that aims at the maintenance of order—'orderly' conduct.[166] The demand for צדקה can thus be understood as the demand for a recognition of the divine order. H.H. Schmid, while referring to Jepsen, defines what he calls the proto-Israelite, Canaanite concept of צדק as the expression of a *world order* (*Weltordnung*), which brings to mind the Egyptian concept of *Ma'at*.[167] Schmid sees the concept of a world order as the fundamental meaning (*Grundbedeutung*) that lies behind the Old Testament usage of צדק, whose semantic tradition history he follows through the different areas where צדק occurs.[168] According to Schmid the Old Testament 'inherits' this concept of a world order from its Canaanite predecessor in the land of Palestine and sets its stamp upon the concept for its own usage.[169] Some of the Canaanite aspects are toned down; the root צדק plays a less significant role in war and cultic terminology and in conjunction with nature and fertility there occurs a clear reinterpretation. On the other hand the root is frequently employed in connection with conceptions of justice, wisdom and the monarchy. Different periods and theologies employ the concept of צדק as an expression for different conditions, and within the individual fields the words receive their different specifications. But throughout there remains a desire for the maintenance of the cosmos. The maintenance of the world order is the goal to which faithfulness to the fellowship is directed.[170]

H.H. Schmid, *Gerechtigkeit als Weltordnung*; B. Mogensen, '*ṣeḏāqā* in the Scandinavian and German Research Traditions'.

166. Cf. Jepsen, 'צדק und צדקה', p. 80. It is not possible to maintain Jepsen's distinction as a general principle, and it has not been generally recognized; but it does at the least reveal that in certain cases it is meaningful to operate with two sets of meaning.

167. H.H. Schmid, *Gerechtigkeit als Weltordnung*, pp. 66ff.

168. The root was originally employed in connection with justice, wisdom, nature/fertility, war/victory over enemies, cult/sacrifice in conjunction with the monarchy (*Gerechtigkeit als Weltordnung*, pp. 14-23). *Ma'at* is found in an Egyptian context within the same sphere of application (*Gerechtigkeit als Weltordnung*, pp. 46-61). An analogous concept, *mē*, is found in Sumerian (*Gerechtigkeit als Weltordnung*, pp. 61-65). Schmid does not use the words 'fundamental meaning' (*Grundbedeutung*) as the expression of an original, unchangeable constancy—the constant sense of צדק is 'order'—that has served as the point of departure for the variable, concrete use of the word, but, on the contrary, as 'the objectified sum of a long conceptual history', where the concrete statement is not a random expression of the ideal basic concept, but is the true manifestation of it. In practice Schmid must concede that the straightforward use of *Grundbedeutung* often imposes itself (*Gerechtigkeit als Weltordnung*, pp. 170-71).

169. Schmid here follows (naturally) the settlement and religio-historical theories of the school of Alt and Noth. In particular he employs the distinction between the Canaanite type of religion and the Israelite *Gott der Väter*, which he without reservations identifies with Yahweh.

170. Koch is more radical in his understanding. In his dissertation he regards צדק as a divine being (*Wesen*) ('Sdq im Alten Testament', p. 15), which descents from God in the cult; later he describes צדק as 'a Sphere, which permanently surrounds him [*sc.* man]. This sphere is of a concrete materiality and belongs to man the same way as his property' ('Gibt es ein Vergeltungsdogma im Alten Testament?', p. 166). Concerning Koch's view, Schmid writes: 'In this sense it is correct: צדק/צדקה also has a relationship to cult and sacrifice. That they are as central to the Old Testament, as Koch claims, is though hardly the case. It cannot be denied that the majority of the cultic examples (in the Psalms of lament) are aimed at a sacral divine court and that thereby צדק is to be understood more in a judicial sense than in a cultic sense' (*Gerechtigkeit als Weltordnung*, p. 22).

What significance does this have for our understanding of צדקה/צדק in the book of Hosea? First of all, that it cannot be a question of random terminology in the few places where the book of Hosea employs the term (2.21; 10.12 along with 14.10 [gloss]). Secondly, that it is hardly safe territory that the prophet occupies when he in 10.12 says that Yahweh will let צדק rain upon the people (ירה II). By all means, there is a certain tendency for the root צדק to be used figuratively in the Old Testament,[171] which Schmid sees as a conscious rejection of the fertility elements in צדקה/צדק. But the significance of this rejection for the 'official' Yahweh theology, which marks the Old Testament texts in their present redactional version, is emphasized precisely by the special affinity between צדק and ideas about nature, fertility and growth,[172] particularly in the popular religiosity. Fertility, too, is dependent upon order.[173] If צדק is synonymous with the superior principle that Yahweh sends as a gift to the righteous person (צדיק), who walks—or sows—in צדקה (that conduct that strives for order), then it is no accident that precisely צדקה is parallel with חסד in Hos. 10.12, and that two different derivative forms of the root צדק are used in the verse. For in the pre-exilic period there is no doubt that the righteous (צדיק) will live (well), while the unrighteous (רשע) will die.[174] It is first with Ezekiel that we encounter serious considerations concerning the possibility that the righteous can jeopardize their righteousness.[175]

The most relevant help for understanding צדקה/צדק in the book of Hosea is found in the Psalms,[176] where Yahweh, beyond being the

171. Otherwise Koch, 'Ṣdq im Alten Testament', p. 50.
172. Cf. Schmid, *Gerechtigkeit als Weltordnung*, pp. 7-18.
173. We also speak today of 'the order of nature' in a nearly hypostatized sense. That the order of nature has a close connection to the royal ideology in the entire ancient Near Eastern area—and in Israel as well, where the king (often as the son of the god) is regarded as responsible for fertility—is an important point, which we do not need to deal with more closely here, but which emphasizes the understanding of צדק as a principle of order.
174. Cf. Schmid, *Gerechtigkeit als Weltordnung*, p. 95.
175. Cf. Schmid, *Gerechtigkeit als Weltordnung*, pp. 126ff.
176. It would seem to be unfortunate that only material from Jerusalem can be cited as providing a background for understanding northern ways of thinking. But with the ancient Near Eastern background in mind, it does however seem reasonable to do so, all the more so given that we have no possibility of knowing with any certainty how much of a difference there is between northern and southern religiosity in the monarchical period. This is due among other things to the simple fact that the

sustainer of the order of nature, is presented especially in the Psalms of lament as the righteous judge, who obtains for the צדיקים, the righteous (= the innocent), the justice that they deserve—and consequently punishes the unrighteous. In this way balance and order in the world that Yahweh rules is maintained.[177] We recognize this absolute contrast between צדק and רשע in Hos. 10.12-13a, too. Another area where the Psalms can shed light upon Hos. 10.12 is in their presentation of צדק as Yahweh's gift to the righteous (צדיק), which K. Koch in particular has called attention to.[178] In Hos. 10.12 it is said that by sending צדק Yahweh sustains that striving after the proper order, that צדקה, in which Israel will sow when it seeks him (דרש) and receives his צדק. In and by the election Israel has thus been enjoined to live in accordance with that order that Yahweh has instituted and the demands that the election makes for an active recognition of Yahweh as the one God.

It seems odd that the third part of v. 12a, נירו לכם ניר, 'break up your fallow ground', apparently does not contain a corresponding religious concept. We must therefore assume that the words נירו לכם ניר in themselves are meaningful enough to serve as a metaphor in the context. We do not receive any help for interpretation from other passages in the Old Testament; but it is likely that the three imperatives in v. 12a all metaphorically designate the right way to live according to Yahweh's election in contrast to the way of living before the election. Thus, to break up fallow ground means 'to live in an entirely new way, to give up the previous way of living'. It is not the case that v. 12a indicates the socially correct method of cultivation—it must be maintained that the language is metaphorical. The emphasis is upon the words צדקה and חסד with their

book of Hosea is the only example we have of genuine northern prophecy, that it is the only writing that we with any certainty *know* is northern, and that the book of Hosea has been redacted and partly re-written in Judah. Moreover, nothing in the book of Hosea speaks against the comparisons made.

177. Cf. Schmid, *Gerechtigkeit als Weltordnung*, pp. 144-54. If we go to the book of Proverbs, the dominant mentality is that of a close connection between deed and result; the רשע inflicts punishment upon himself (cf. Koch, 'Gibt es ein Vergeltungsdogma im Alten Testament?', pp. 131-40). Koch also finds a corresponding way of thinking in the Psalms. It is often, however, modified in the sense that Yahweh is the one who puts into effect the fate that resides in the deed. On the other hand, there is no such thing as retributive *punishment* (Koch, 'Gibt es ein Vergeltungsdogma im Alten Testament?', pp. 148-56).

178. See above nn. 164 and 169.

strong stress upon the close connection with Yahweh.[179]

Verse 12b remains within the realm of the metaphors provided by agriculture and rain in 12a—and the verse remains within the area of Canaanite mythology. The copula ו indicates that Yahweh must be sought while at the same time performing the three tasks mentioned.[180] Seeking (דרש) Yahweh in order to pray to him is part of the true relationship to God. Or, as Kinet expresses it,

> Verse 12 thus describes Israel's task as an exclusive orientation towards Yahweh: Israel must live and work in such a way that it thereby meets the requirements of the relationship to Yahweh.[181]

Thus Hosea does not use random categories when he describes the relationship to Yahweh. צדק/צדקה and חסד are Yahweh-theological key words—and contradict the worship that is described in v. 13a (see below, pp. 96-97). The statement that Yahweh lets צדק rain upon the people (12bβ) has the same function, for according to Canaanite religion it is Baal who causes fertility to come by means of the rain.[182] When Hosea in 10.12 indeed uses fertility terms together with terms that are constitutive for the concept דעת אלהים (cf. 6.6), he is thereby able to sharpen the contrast between vv. 12 and 13a as much as possible. This is emphasized further by the fact that צדק with its popular religious, divine connotations is brought together with the verb ירה II.

---

179. Another emphasis is found in F. Reiterer, *Gerechtigkeit als Heil*, pp. 149-53. Reiterer examines the use of צדק/צדקה in the book of Hosea, in that he includes the concepts משפט, חסד, רחמים, אמונה and דעת (2.21-22), which are used by the prophet 'in the same breath' to present the 'order of life (*Lebensordnung*), love, and experience of God' (p. 151). צדק belongs to the same group. As far as the use of the term in 10.12-13a is concerned, צדקה has the same meaning as that which Reiterer finds to be true for Proverbs, namely, 'the behaviour (as deed and/or as attitude) of the people' (p. 153). This צדקה should imply that the people treat each other decently and properly. If they do so, then Yahweh will send his צדק. 10.12a and 13a deal, therefore, with 'interpersonal behaviour in Israel' (*ibid.*). With the use of the parallel concept חסד, there is added 'a dimension of intimacy and inwardness'. Reiterer lays (in my view incorrectly) greater stress on interpersonal ethics than on the relationship to God in his description of צדק and in his overall interpretation of the verse. This is related to an insufficient understanding of רשע and עולתה, in which, according to Reiterer, 'the aspect of faithful belongingness to Yahweh is not included' (*ibid.*).

180. Kinet, *Ba'al und Jahwe*, p. 327 n. 64.

181. Kinet, *Ba'al und Jahwe*, p. 173.

182. See in this regard Kapelrud, *Baal in the Ras Shamra Texts*, pp. 93-98.

Results

All things considered Hos. 10.12 deals with the proper relationship to God, presented in the categories of the fertility cult, but with the content of an 'orthodox' Yahweh faith.[183] Hosea is also here playing with Canaanite fire, but not in as marked a fashion as some have previously believed, especially in Anglo–Scandinavian scholarship.

In v. 13a comes the disclosure of the people's disobedience. They have not obeyed the command to live a life in the service of Yahweh, but they have in fact lived in opposition to Yahweh's command: רשע is in diametrical opposition to צדקה, and עולתה and כחש are its consequences. J. Schreiner expresses it in this way:

> The action and the conditions (*Tun und Ergehen*) that follow thereupon correspond to one another. Hosea (10.13) makes use of the image of sowing and harvesting in order to say that out of wickedness (רשע) comes unrighteousness (עולתה) and deception (כחש), and thus demonstrates that an attitude, which in the eyes of God is not in order, produces deeds of injustice and does not lead to the expected success.[184]

The ideas are not conveyed directly in the pericope 10.11-13a. The statement about their actions remains open, but is not to be mistaken as anything other than opposition to Yahweh's demand. The explanation comes first in the following statement, 10.13b-15, which the redaction has connected to 10.11-13a. Hos. 10.11-13a uses the language of fertility metaphors to describe Israel as Yahweh's chosen people, a people who from the beginning had their own worth, but who have refused to fulfil the task that Yahweh had destined them for, namely to serve him. The election's precise historical circumstances lie beyond the scope of the pericope, which is why it cannot be used to prove the existence of a finding tradition or of a settlement tradition. It bears witness to the fact *that* Israel was elected, not *how* the election occurred.

183. 'Orthodox' is essentially a misleading word, in that it suggests the existence of an underlying ancient monotheistic Yahweh faith. But rather than being seen as restorative figures, the 'writing prophets' ought to be regarded as reforming and renewing. This was the view of Wellhausen, presented in *Prolegomena zur Geschichte Israels*, and this view has recently been taken up for reconsideration. See, for example, Lemche, *Ancient Israel*, pp. 209-10; and cf. below Chapter 4, Section B.

184. Schreiner, 'עול'. Notice how צדקה and רשע are placed in parallel fashion in vv. 12 and 13a. Concerning the contrast between the two concepts, see further, for example, Jepsen, 'צדק und צדקה', p. 82. Notice, moreover, how Schreiner speaks about עולתה as the expression of an action that 'is not in *order*' (my emphasis); compare the definition above of צדקה/צדק as the expression of a principle of order.

E. *Yahweh's People—The Chosen People*

We have now investigated the traditions in the book of Hosea that are concerned with Yahweh's election of the people of his possession and have found that this election took place in the 'historical' sphere. But this state of affairs does not mean that one could speak about one particular election. The election could be described as something that took place almost previous to history (in Egypt), in the wilderness, and after the settlement. *This election resulted in Yahweh's demand for exclusivity on Israel.*

We have not found any trace of the concluding of a covenant in connection with the demand for exclusivity. Hosea does indeed employ the covenant metaphor, but without mentioning any event in conjunction with the concluding of a covenant. In Hos. 6.7 the covenant is in fact a picture of Yahweh's historically based legal claim upon Israel— that claim that the people refused to obey, when 'they transgressed the covenant at Adam'. The breaking of the covenant is a break with Yahweh's demand for exclusivity. The conclusion of the investigations in Section A was indeed also that one (against Wolff, among others) cannot presuppose the existence of a covenantal theology as a framework for understanding the book of Hosea, but that one on the other hand (against Perlitt) does not need to reject totally the idea that Hosea could speak about Israel's relationship to God as a covenant.

We have seen that Hosea (and the Hosea tradents) were able to draw upon certain already existing 'historical' or mythical traditions in the exposition of Yahweh's and Israel's relationship to one another, a relationship based on the demand for exclusivity. In Chapter 2 we examined the image of Jacob and its use in Hosea 12, and in this chapter we have seen how the call from Egypt (11.1) or the sojourn in the wilderness (12.10; 13.4) was assumed as being well known by the audience. Thus, there existed traditions about Israel's history previous to Hosea, but we cannot with certainty identify them, in that we do not have the necessary written materials at our disposal. One is, therefore, limited to arguing for the existence of oral traditions, probably of a more narrative character than we find them in the book of Hosea. It is, of course, completely unrealistic to try to find the oral wording of these traditions on the basis of an analysis of the exposition presented in the book of Hosea.

The demand for exclusivity is in Hosea grounded in the mythical-durative, in contrast to the Deuteronomistic covenant's character of a unique historical event.[185] This election is most often presented as a metaphor, and among these metaphors the picture of how Yahweh found Israel in the wilderness has attracted special interest. We have previously touched upon—albeit sporadically—the finding tradition, and we will deal with this theory more closely in Part II, where we will investigate the so-called finding motif with regard to its extent, content and use in the book of Hosea, together with the influence that this tradition formation has had on later Old Testament.

---

185. Modern research shows, however, that prior to Deuteronomistic theology there are different covenant agreements, which all have the purpose of guaranteeing Israel's status at the people of God. See in this regard Nicholson, *God and his People*, pp. 148ff.

Part II

PROPHETIC TRADITION

Chapter 4

ELECTION THEOLOGY UNTIL HOSEA—AN EXPERIMENT

It has already been established at several points in this study that Hosea's theology is based on a conception about election and exclusivity. Yahweh's demand is founded in history, Israel must know this history, the priests ought to proclaim it, and Israel should be loyal to it. The election is described as something that took place either in Egypt, or in the wilderness, or in the cultivated land. These three places are not necessarily alternatives, for the election is a recurring event. Or more precisely, it *was* a recurring event, for Hosea also proclaims that the people no longer can or will receive the election. They worship Baal (whom they believe is the same god as Yahweh), they rely on their own power, and the priests and the leaders disregard Yahweh's teaching and order. But Hosea also proclaims the possibility of salvation. Yahweh will one day lead his people through the wilderness and restore the relationship; he will one day heal their apostasy.

A. *'Hoseas Geistige Heimat'*
Hans Walther Wolff's Interpretation Critically Examined

The Background
Where does Hosea's Election Theology come from? It was demonstrated in Chapter 2 that there was an influence from the cult. Hos. 12.6 ('Yahweh, the God of Hosts, Yahweh is his name') was found to be a doxology that was borrowed from the cult (see above, pp. 40-41). The formula in 12.10 and 13.4 also received a cultic determination, namely what Zimmerli has designated as the so-called 'formula of self-presentation' (*Selbsvorstellungsformel*; see above, pp. 61-62). This formula has its greatest impact in the priestly literature (The Holiness Code) and can be traced forward in time as well (Ezekiel, Deutero-Isaiah). Its cultic usage is attested by Psalms 50 and 81, two psalms that

cannot be dated with certainty, but that in any case cannot be earlier than the eighth century.

It would thus appear that we find the first written result of the formula in the book of Hosea. But that fact simply means that we do not have earlier written sources for the formula. It does not mean that Hosea has 'invented' the formula or that it has been interpolated. On the contrary, its cultic *Sitz im Leben* gives rise to the possibility that the formula had a long history prior to its use by Hosea. While it is not our task here to try to follow the history of this tradition, it is however important to observe how Hosea makes use of such 'borrowed goods'. We have correspondingly already seen how he does so in the discussion of Hos. 5.8–6.6 and 10.11-13a, where cultic material is also employed, albeit from the cult of Baal.

It has often been claimed that Hosea—as well as the other writing prophets—was hostile to the cult or at least critical of it. But it has been argued previously in this monograph that Hosea's task consisted among other things of a cleansing of the cult as well as of a restoration of the legitimate priestly tasks. We have among other things seen how he seeks to reform the cult in Bethel from the worship of the calf idol (10.5) to the original Yahweh cult as initiated by Jacob (see pp. 43-46). And we have seen how the liturgical and historical utterances go together and form part of a joint exposition of the demand for exclusivity (12.3-7, 10-11; 13.4-6).

This observation is less surprising if we remind ourselves that it was precisely the clergy that was intended to have the role of mediator of theological knowledge, דעת אלהים, for the people.

'Hoseas Geistige Heimat'—A Discussion with Hans Walther Wolff

Hans Walther Wolff claims that דעת אלהים is preserved in certain esoteric circles to which Hosea also belonged. This view is set forth in his article, 'Hoseas geistige Heimat' ('Hosea's Spiritual Home').

On the basis of Hos. 6.4-6; 9.7-9; 12.8-11 and 12.13-15 (he regards 4.5a as a Judaean gloss) Wolff claims that 'Hosea knows that he is not only related to previous prophets, but also to prophetic circles of his own day' and that 'he sees himself allied with them in opposition to the present-day official Israel and its cult' (p. 243). Hosea's occupation with the cult and history is, however, not explained by these connections alone.[1] He shares these concerns with the Levitical priestly circles, which

---

1. One cannot with any seriousness label the prophetic circles, as they are known

were in opposition to the official Israel and its cult (p. 245), and Wolff claims that the basic features of Hosea's proclamation are incomprehensible without recognizing their basis in a 'community of opposition' composed of priests and Levites. Wolff sees the existence of such a community confirmed by Hosea's use of special traditions such as the finding tradition (p. 240) and the Deuteronomic program, which in fact would have its roots in this community.

Wolff's understanding of the situation is not without problems. The possibility that prophetic-levitical circles should have been an 'amphictyonic oriented community' (p. 250) has in fact been rejected by recent research concerning the probability of the existence of the amphictyony. Our confidence in the historical veracity of the reports that Wolff bases his conclusions on has been shaken.[2]

As far as Hosea's criticism of the cult is concerned, which he supposedly shared with this oppositional circle, it would appear that Wolff's notions in this regard are somewhat exaggerated. The theme of Hosea's criticism of the cult has already undergone to an exegetical treatment (see above, pp. 43-46). In agreement with Grace Emmerson, I there maintained that Hosea does not reject Bethel as 'evil', but on the contrary attempts to reform the old Yahweh place of worship so that it 'again' becomes a place of true worship. All things considered, Hosea does not set forth a general rejection of the sacrificial cult. This can be seen, for example, in 9.4, where the prohibition against sacrificing is indeed a part of the punishment. Therefore Hos. 6.6 cannot be used to support the claim of absolute animosity to the cult as Wolff does.[3]

---

to us from the Northern Kingdom, as 'bearers of cultic customs and protectors of sacred tradition' ('Hoseas geistige Heimat', p. 244).

2.   Thus 1 Kgs 12.31 is not modified first and foremost by the remark in Judg. 18.30, as Wolff claims, but on the contrary by the ideology of cult centralization in the Deuteronomistic History. The story in Exod. 32, which portrays the Levites as Moses' henchmen, does not precede Hosea's proclamation but is its result, and Exod. 32.25-29 is even presumably to be regarded as an insertion in the story (E. Aurelius, *Der Fürbitter Israels*, p. 76 and pp. 66-67). And we are no longer able to speak without reservations about Ahija, Elijah, Elisha and Micaiah ben Imlah as names that 'belong to the *history* of the Northern Kingdom' (p. 235, my emphasis): see, for example, with regard to Micaiah ben Imlah, Würthwein, 'Zur Komposition von 1 Reg 22.1-38'.

3.   Wolff, 'Hoseas geistige Heimat', p. 235: 'The contemporary priesthood maintained a cult with sacrificial and burnt offerings. The prophets, on the other hand, were those instruments of Yahweh, who, through the announcement of judgment,

The prophets relationship to the cult is a 'classic theme' in prophetic research. The question was formulated by Ernst Würthwein in the terms of two key ideas: are the so-called anticultic statements by the prophets *Kultpolemik*, that is, polemic against the cult as such, and matters of principle, or are they *Kultbescheid*, topical critique and a response to particular problems in the present-day cult? That they are *Kultpolemik* was urged, for example, by Paul Volz;[4] that they are *Kultbescheid* is argued by Würthwein himself.[5] In her PhD lecture Kirsten Nielsen[6] by means of an analysis of Isa. 1.2-20 arrives at an interpretation according to which

> the general repudiation...naturally does not deal with the cult as such, as Volz believed, but with any and every attempt in a *situation where the covenant has been broken* to try to come to terms with Yahweh by means of cultic compensation. The radical nature of the repudiation is to be found here (this radical repudiation was clearly perceived by Volz, but interpreted incorrectly), but here is also to be found the basic validity of the repudiation.[7]

As far as Hosea is concerned in any case, this claim requires one modification. Hosea does not speak about a breach of the covenant in a way that was assumed to be the case just 20 years ago. Hosea's point of departure is the demand for exclusivity; the point of departure for Yahweh's repudiation of the cult is that the people have not lived up to this demand. This is why it is not the sacrificial cult, but חסד and דעת אלהים that are demanded, because, as we have previously noted, precisely these two concepts give expression to the recognition of the demand for exclusivity. When such recognition is lacking, Yahweh withdraws from the people (Hos. 5.6; see above, pp. 86-88).

The connection between Wolff's perception of Hosea's relationship to

would demonstrate again that divine justice and the spirit of the covenant were the genuine will of Yahweh, as it should be maintained in Israel through a knowledge of God that was both proclaimed and taken to heart'.

4.   P. Volz, 'Die radikale Ablehnung der Kultreligion durch die alttestamentlichen Propheten'.

5.   E. Würthwein, 'Kultpolemik oder Kultbescheid? Tradition und Situation'.

6.   K. Nielsen, 'Profeternes opgør med kulten'. Here she summarizes the positions of Volz: 'While cultic religion—the religion of the priesthood—attempted to build a tower of Babel in order to pave a way for itself to heaven by means of cultic measures, the prophets proclaimed the unique rule of the exalted God', and of Würthwein: 'In the anti-cultic statements it is not a question of a polemic against the cult in principle, but of a topical critique of a specific cultic violation', *ibid.*, pp. 218, 219.

7.   'Profeternes opgør med kulten', p. 229 (Nielsen's emphasis).

the cult and that of Volz is obvious and does require further elaboration. The main lines of Würthwein's understanding, as it is further developed here by Kirsten Nielsen, provide a far more fruitful understanding of the problem. Seen against this background and in the light of Hos. 9.15 (see above, pp. 68-70) it is likely that Emmerson is right when she claims that

> [Hos.] 6.6 is not to be understood as a total rejection of sacrifice. The contrast is posed starkly between חסד and זבח for emphasis, and is not to be taken in an absolute sense as the parallel expression, knowledge of God rather than[8] burnt offerings indicates.[9]

Hosea's thinking is along the same lines as that represented clearly at a later date in the Temple Sermon in Jeremiah 7, namely, that sacrifice without faith is worthless.[10] Or as Emmerson puts it: 'In the context of a right relationship with God sacrifice has a legitimate place'.[11]

We must therefore conclude that Hosea's criticism of the cult is directed *partly* against the cult of the wrong god, that is, Baal instead of Yahweh, and *partly* against a cult founded on an erroneous basis: by means of the cultivation of Baal the people have neglected the demand for exclusivity.

The absolute distinction that Wolff makes between Hosea's prophetic friends and those prophets who are a part of the state administration or between Hosea and the surrounding society must be a cause for misgivings. It would appear that Wolff is here still under the influence of the individualism of the nineteenth century's German Liberal Theology that regards the prophets as solitary individuals who stand over against the 'comatose' society. Bernhard Lang, on the contrary, urges that the prophetic office—also the 'free, charismatic' forms—belong to a particular tradition and—what is important—must be seen as strongly defined by the surrounding society.[12] The political aspect of prophecy lies beyond the scope of the present study, but it can be mentioned here in

---

8.   מן is here to be understood not as a privative but as expressing comparison' (Emmerson, *Hosea*, p. 198 n. 161).

9.   Emmerson, *Hosea*, p. 153 with n. 161. It is in addition Emmerson's opinion that 'It is clear, on the other hand, that criticism of Israel's cult was prominent in Hosea's message, and, on the other, very probable that powerful influences in Judah have, deliberately or inadvertently, shaped the present form of the material' (*Hosea*, pp. 119-20).

10.   See in this regard Kragelund, *Fra profeti til prædiken*, pp. 532-33.

11.   Emmerson, *Hosea*.

12.   Lang, *Monotheism and the Prophetic Minority*, especially ch. 2, 'What is a Prophet?', and ch. 3, 'The Making of Prophets in Israel'.

order to shed light on how Hosea participated in the surrounding society and its religious institutions. Hosea did not—as a kind of John the Baptist figure—turn his back completely on society and its religious institutions. Even the prophetic call itself presupposes a psychological openness for a tradition, or rather, as Lang notes in agreement with the Swedish psychologist of religion Hjalmar Sundén,[13] the call follows a willed and learned familiarity with the way in which one becomes a prophet.

Wolff is still, therefore, right about the fact that Hosea was most likely connected with prophetic circles; but this does not necessarily mean that these circles were in principle opposed to cultic life. Such an idea is, as far as that goes, only comprehensible on the basis of a Protestant emphasis on individual faith as opposed to a collective liturgical understanding of worship.

As far as the idea of a Levitical element in Hosea's 'spiritual home' is concerned, Wolff has here received his inspiration from von Rad's *Deuteronomiumstudien*.[14] According to von Rad, Deuteronomy's pre-history is indeed to be found in northern, Levitical circles.[15] We cannot

---

13. H. Sundén, *Die Religion und die Rollen*. A sociological investigation of prophets is also found, for example, in D.L. Petersen, *The Roles of Israel's Prophets*. He also underscores the prophet's societal role, in that he regards this role in relationship to chronology and organization. He sees the term נביא as exclusively Northern and defines the נביא as a 'covenant spokesman', while the Southern prophetic type, חזה, is designated as 'a herald from the divine council to humanity'. The societal background for these two types is respectively the Northern, disparate tribal society and the Southern centralized state (ch. 5). But both prophetic types belong to the role of 'central minority prophets' (see in this regard pp. 66-68). Petersen provides a *corrigendum* to Lang's understanding of the conditional nature of the prophetic call when he points out that 'central morality prophecy' as distinguished from earlier forms of prophecy is 'actively limited to a few individuals'. Thus Petersen regards Isaiah's disciples (Isa. 8.16) as being on the same line as Jeremiah's 'amanuensis' Baruch and not as genuine בני הנביאים (*ibid.*).

14. Wolff mentions in addition A. Bentzen, *Die josianische Reform und ihre Voraussetzungen*, pp. 46ff., and F. Horst, *Das Privilegrecht Jahwes*, p. 123 (cf. Wolff, 'Hoseas geistige Heimat', p. 248 n. 65).

15. In *Deuteronomiumstudien* von Rad regards the Deuteronomistic movement as a reform movement, building on the traditions of the ancient Yahweh amphictyony, which they wished to revive. The basis for this movement is 'the free peasant rural population', which has kept 'the ancient patriarchal traditions of the strict Yahweh-faith' (p. 46). The movement's real spokesmen are the Judaean rural Levites, and it is among them that we find the authors of Deuteronomy. At a later date, von Rad concurs, however, with the views of Alt and Wolff and places the origin of

in the present context touch upon the problem of the origins of Deuteronomy. In any case, Deuteronomy's origins are to be found at a later time than Hosea's use of traditional materials.[16] Indeed, as Wolff believes,[17] the rise of Deuteronomy is dependent upon Hosea's use of traditions. Deuteronomy's theology can therefore hardly be employed as an argument for a Levitical *background* for Hosea. Should it be the case that the Levitical element is decisive for Deuteronomy, which is by no means an undisputed question,[18] then it is the Deuteronomic circle that is dependent upon Hosean theology, and by this is meant the theology that was 'Hosea's spiritual home'.

Yet another objection should be noted, namely that von Rad's (and Wolff's) portrayal of the orthodox rural Levite, who was an enthusiastic supporter of the amphictyony and mediated his knowledge of the תורה to others, belongs to another, and much later, period than Hosea's.

It is difficult in the recent scholarly world to see any enthusiasm for the idea of the primitive amphictyony since the fall of the 'amphictyony dogma'. And the figure of the Levitical teacher depends upon von Rad's understanding of Deuteronomy's complex structure, which in his view can only have its origin in the (Levitical) priesthood at Shechem.[19] If we take a look at von Rad's earlier work, we can see that the Levitical preaching, which is characterized by the 're-use' of older scriptural passages, is determined to be post-exilic. In his studies of Chronicles,[20] he demonstrates how the sermons there reflect Levitical preaching, whose *Sitz-im-Leben* is to be found 'among those Levites who had been dismissed from their positions because of the centralization of the cult' and who 'had found their sphere of activity in religious instruction'.[21]

Deuteronomy in the Northern Kingdom because of—among other things—the affinity with Hosea (*Das fünfte Buch Mose*—Deuteronomium, pp. 18-19).

16. Cf. von Rad, *Deuteronomiumstudien*, p. 48.

17. 'Hoseas geistige Heimat', p. 249, in agreement with A. Alt, 'Die Heimat des Deuteronomiums'.

18. The theory that Northern Levitical circles were the point of departure for the Deuteronomistic movement carries with it the drawback that we find in Deuteronomy a description of the Levites as *personae miserabiles* (see, for example, Deut. 14.29), a difficulty that von Rad is aware of but rejects. Another difficulty is the question about what interest the Levites might have had in a centralization of the cult in Jerusalem.

19. Von Rad, *Deuteronomiumstudien*, pp. 47-48 and in this regard M. Weinfeld, *Deuteronomy and the Deuteronomic School*, pp. 56-57.

20. Von Rad, 'Die levitische Predigt in den Büchern der Chronik'.

21. Von Rad, 'Die levitische Predigt in den Büchern der Chronik', pp. 258-59.

As far as the northern origins of the Levites is concerned, two things should be noted: (1) that von Rad in his *Studies in Deuteronomy* naturally assumes their Judaean provenance, and (2) that this position has recently been taken up again and rejected by Miller and Hayes. They assign the Levitical priesthood to the regions around Bethlehem and believe that David employed Levites extensively in his administration.[22] The previous 'rural parish clerk' thus fades from view and with it Wolff's 'oppositional congregation' as well.[23]

B. *'Hosea's Spiritual Home': The Yahweh-Alone Movement*

Hosea and the Priesthood

With all this in mind, where do we then find 'Hosea's spiritual home?' That he had such a home is beyond dispute, for we have seen in Chapters 2 and 3 above how he took over previous material and made use of it. My proposition is that *Hosea was familiar with the traditions that had been transmitted in the temples among the priests.* But isn't this understanding contradicted by the speech against the priests in Hos. 4.4-10?

4   Yet let no one contend,
      and let none accuse,
      but my people stand as an accusation against you, O Priest.
5   You shall stumble by day
      as my people also stumble by night,
      and I will destroy your tribe.
6   My people are destroyed, because they lack knowledge.
      Because you have rejected knowledge
      I reject you from being a priest to me.
      You have forgotten the teaching of your God,
      so I will also forget your sons.

See in addition Weinfeld, *Deuteronomy and the Deuteronomic School*, p. 54.

22. Miller and Hayes, *A History of Ancient Israel and Judah*, p. 113.

23. The picture of the Levite as an oppositional figure presumably depends upon Deuteronomy's representation of him as *persona miserabilis* (see above, n. 18). There has been an ongoing debate concerning the origin of the tribe of Levi: the etymology of the name Levi, the question as to whether there was a secular tribe of Levi, the relationship to Moses and the Ark. See in this regard, for example, E. Nielsen, *Shechem*, pp. 264-83; *idem*, 'The Levites in Ancient Israel'; A.H.J. Gunneweg, *Leviten und Priester*; a startling suggestion is set forth by G. Schmitt, 'Der Ursprung des Levitentums': the Levites were originally Moses' personal bodyguards.

7   The more they increased, the more they sinned against me;
     I will change their glory into shame.
8   They feed on the sin of my people,
     they are greedy for their iniquity.
9   And it shall be like people, like priest;
     I will pay them back for their ways
     and repay them for their deeds.
10   They shall eat, but not be satisfied;
     they shall play the whore, but not multiply.
     Because they have forsaken Yahweh
     to devote themselves to whoredom and wine.[24]

Hos. 4.1-3 forms the general introduction to the book of Hosea's second major part, Hos. 4-14. Presumably it stems from circles of disciples (*Schülerkreise*),[25] and it is in any case to be regarded as a later summarizing introduction to the following collection.[26] After the introduction there follows a major section (4.4–5.7) in which the overriding theme is the knowledge of God and its antithesis, namely the people's whoring that leads them away from God. In the pericope 4.4-10 the responsibility for this is placed upon the priests. Yahweh himself will not accuse them; this is not necessary, for the deeds of the people, which are explicated in 4.11-14a, are accusation enough (4.4). Since the priests have forgotten their tasks, the people have devoted themselves to the cultivation of idols: 'A people without understanding comes to ruin', as it is said in 4.14b. Therefore Yahweh will punish the priests as well as the people (4.9-10).

There has been some discussion about whether the speech in 4.4-10 is directed towards the priesthood as such[27] or towards a particular priesthood or a particular priest. Wolff holds to the latter opinion, and on the basis of his thesis that Hosea 4–11 and 12–14 are constructed from the so-called 'sketches of scenes' (*Auftrittsskizzen*), believes that this particular episode took place 'in one of the important high places on the mountains of Ephraim', most probably Bethel.[28] With a point of

---

24. The translation with textual criticism on the whole follows that of H. Balz-Cochois, *Gomer*, pp. 22-37, to which the reader is referred.
25. J. Jeremias, 'Hosea 4–7. Beobachtungen zur Komposition des Buches Hosea', p. 49. Otherwise Rudolph, who sees 4.1-10 as one section (*Hosea*, pp. 98-99).
26. Good, 'The Composition of Hosea', p. 30.
27. Rudolph, *Hosea*, p. 102; H. Junker, 'Textkritische, formkritische und traditionsgeschichtliche Untersuchungen zu Os 4,1-10', pp. 168-69.
28. Wolff, *Hosea*, pp. xxx, 76.

departure in the references to 'mother' (4.5) and 'sons' (4.6) he believes that it must be a question of 'the figure of a high priest at one of the major shrines as was the case of Amaziah of Bethel (Amos 7.10)...'[29] Following Rudolph's conjecture, H. Balz-Cochois points out in this regard that such a supposition is rendered superfluous if we read אֶמִּיךְ instead of אִמֶּךָ in 4.5b: 'I will destroy your tribe'. כֹהֵן must then also be understood collectively rather than as referring to a single priest. This understanding fits in well with that period's dialectical perception of the relationship between the individual and the collective. 'The entire clan is always addressed along with the individual, and the respective individual is always addressed together with the clan'. In this way Balz-Cochois can also quite simply explain why the form of address in the prophetic speech in 4.4-10 switches back and forth between 2nd/3rd person singular and 2nd/3rd person plural.[30]

In addition Balz-Cochois believes that she is able to conclude that Hosea is not speaking at the state shrine at Bethel, '...but at some provincial cultic high place'.[31] She supports this statement by referring to the fact that הָאָרֶץ in Hos. 1.2 and 4.1 does not mean the land as a geopolitical entity but rather indicates the cultivated land. 'The "people" are also the pagans'.[32] Balz-Cochois's argument for this latter statement is not convincing, especially when two things are taken into consideration: (1) the thematic and literary distance between chs. 1–3 and 4–14; and (2) that 4.1-3 cannot (against Balz-Cochois) be understood as forming a whole with 4.4-10, but on the contrary is a superscription: 4.1-3 is a thematic introduction to the larger complex.

Other factors ought therefore be taken into consideration if we are going to be able to determine the addressee(s) in Hos. 4.4-10. In my view the pericope ought to be understood in the same way as the so-called 'cultic announcement' (*Kultbescheid*; see above, pp. 103-104), that is, it is a concrete address made in a concrete situation. We must therefore assume that it is directed towards a specific priesthood. Wolff's suggestion, that it is the priesthood at the state shrine at Bethel that is being

29. Wolff, *Hosea*, p. 77. The idea is further developed by Lohfink, 'Zu Text und Form von Os 4,4-6', pp. 308ff., who claims to be able to find a so-called 'three generational pattern'. This is rejected by Rudolph, *Hosea*, pp. 97, 102; Balz-Cochois, *Gomer*, p. 27.
30. Balz-Cochois, *Gomer*, p. 27.
31. Balz-Cochois, *Gomer*, p. 27.
32. Balz-Cochois, *Gomer*, p. 57.

addressed, is attractive, especially in view of the reference to the speech about this shrine in Hosea 12 (see in this regard Chapter 2). But this is and must remain a supposition. We must be satisfied with maintaining that it is a Yahweh-priesthood that is spoken to in a concrete context, and that it is an influential priesthood, since it can be accused of 'the deeds of the people' (4.4). Balz-Cochois's placing of the oracle at some provincial shrine is therefore not convincing.

The speech reels off a string of sins of omission and their consequences. Hosea has apparently believed that he was entitled to blame the priest-hood for not having carried out what amounted to its genuine task, namely, to instruct the people about דעת אלהים.[33] But on this basis we cannot conclude that another priesthood, composed of the Levites and opposed to the state priesthood, stands behind him. *Either* the demand concerning the instruction of the people is utterly new—and what role do the Levites then play for Hosea?—*or also* Hosea is reminding the priests about a task that in his view was already that of the Yahweh-priests, but which they have neglected. In this case the Levites are totally superfluous as transmitters of tradition.

The idea that Hosea reintroduces an old demand could be said to be supported by that knowledge of the contents of the traditions that Hosea could assume for his audience, lay as well as clerical (cf. Chapters 2 and 3). But it is precisely in the statements about the negligence of the priests that we find the key to a better understanding, for although the people are familiar with the 'letter' of the traditions, they do not know their 'spirit'. They are lacking in the knowledge of the demands that are found in the traditions, and herein lies the negligence of the priests. We shall return to this problem later.

Hosea most certainly does, therefore, criticise the priests and pass judgment upon their neglect. But this does not mean that he dissociates himself from the cult and the priesthood as such.

It is not necessary, therefore, to presuppose the existence of an ortho-dox 'oppositional congregation' (*Oppositionsgemeinde*) as a necessary background for understanding Hosea—in any case, not in the form that Wolff imagines.[34] It is more likely that such a group was to be found

---

33. As to whether the accusation is just is another matter, which is considered by Balz-Cochois, *Gomer*, p. 54. In addition, see below, pp. 112-15.

34. Does it not seem likely that the sharp contrast between prophets and priests, which this century's research (largely influenced by Protestantism) takes for granted,

among Hosea's body of followers, who must be reckoned as the first gatherers and tradents of his theology in whatever fashion this may have taken place. But this group must not be confused with a 'spiritual home' (*eine geistige Heimat*). We are able to infer that Hosea had a thorough and firsthand knowledge of what in fact went on in the temples, and that *he criticizes the cult from within.*

Hosea demonstrates a detailed familiarity with the priestly forms of expression of which he makes use. We have already seen how he employs a particular cultic genre (*Gattung*) in Hos. 6.1-6 (see above, p. 83). Hos. 5.1-7 is designated by Balz-Cochois as a 'little Levitical sermon', whose content (kerygma) is that 'cultic impurity is sickness unto death'.[35] Hosea, *the prophet*, feels that he has been called to pass a *priestly* judgment upon Israel/Ephraim's cultic impurity (5.3).[36] Yet another argument for the idea that Hosea's background is to be located in the temple cult is found in his use of language and metaphor. We have already on several occasions touched upon the fact that Hosea makes use of language that is closely related to the Baal cult. I have described this use of language as bold in that it easily can lead to misunderstandings and yet again to a mistaken identification between Baal and Yahweh—and that is precisely what Hosea wishes to oppose.

At this point, we must now ask whether Hosea had any choice. First of all, the cultic language of the shrines of the high places, with its religiosity that is anything but monotheistic, is in fact *the language available with which one can speak about God.* Secondly, it is that religious language that the audience knew and understood. As we have seen, it is not a question of there having been two kinds of shrines, the orthodox Yahweh-shrines and all of the other abominable temples for idols. Yahweh existed side by side with the rest of the Northwest Semitic pantheon. It is this situation that Hosea is attempting to combat, but for this struggle he has no other weapons than the existing religious ideas, which he must make use by turning them upside down. Hosea was not able to make use of 'pure' words that were faithful to Yahweh. He had to work the material that was at hand.[37]

---

is a product of a pietistic and individualistic type of worshipper, which has nothing to do with the Northwest Semitic situation?

35. Balz-Cochois, *Gomer*, p. 70.

36. Balz-Cochois, *Gomer*, p. 66.

37. Something similar can be observed with regard to other great reformers, for example, Paul.

Hosea and the Yahweh-Alone Movement

This perception of Hosea's situation is also found in the work of Morton Smith and Bernhard Lang, who together with Hermann Vorländer have published the composite work, *Der Einzige Gott: Die Geburt des biblischen Monotheismus* (*'The only God: The Birth of Biblical Monotheism'*). The subtitle indicates quite clearly what is at issue: Israelite-Jewish monotheism does not stem from an original primeval monotheism, but is on the contrary the final stage in a development away from general Western Semitic polytheism. In the foreword to the book the editor, B. Lang, expresses the position as follows.[38]

> The authors of this book wish to present a particular point of view, which can be summarized as follows:
>
> 1. The most ancient religion in Israel is—as is the case for the other peoples of the Ancient Near Eastern World—polytheistic, i.e., the people worshipped a multiplicity of gods and goddesses.
>
> 2. Neither the patriarchs Abraham, Isaac and Jacob nor Moses are to be regarded as the adherents of a monotheistic religion or even of a religion similar to monotheism. The view set forth in the late 18th century by Friedrich Schiller, in the 19th century by August Comte, and in the 20th century by Sigmund Freud that the biblical belief in one God stems from a particular stream of ancient Egyptian religiosity is rejected.
>
> 3. During the monarchical period in ancient Israel and especially after the eighth century BCE, the demand that Yahweh—the ancient Israelite national god—alone should be worshipped to the exclusion of the other deities is to be found in certain circles.
>
> 4. During the period of the Babylonian Exile (sixth century BCE) the exclusive worship of Yahweh was further developed into monotheism, in that the existence of all of the heathen gods was denied. With the emergence of a stateless Judaism, which replaced the monarchical Israel, the intolerant belief in one God entered world history. Since then little has changed, and it has until today determined the confession of faith of the great western religions (…).[39]

As mentioned, this understanding of the basic lines of the development of Israel's faith in Yahweh is shared by the present writer. To be sure I am unable to accept the book's unexpressed assumption of the validity of the classical theory concerning the occupation of the land,[40] but the

---

38. The book contains the following contributions: M. Smith, 'Religiöse Parteien bei den Israeliten vor 587'; B. Lang, 'Die Jahwe-allein-Bewegung'; H. Vorländer, 'Der Monotheismus Israels als Antwort auf die Krise des Exils'.

39. Lang, *Der einzige Gott*, pp. 7-8.

40. It is problematic that current presentations of the history of Israel's religion

main point in this context is elsewhere, namely that Israel's faith for centuries was concerned with a far greater spectrum of divinities than the Old Testament is interested in presenting. The Old Testament is, if not written, then at least *redacted, adapted, and censured* by the winning 'party', what in Morton Smith's terminology is designated as the so-called 'Yahweh-Alone party'.[41] But the final victory of this party came at a far later time than that of Hosea, and, if one is going to find his background, then one must hermeneutically seek to disclaim the point of view of the Yahweh-Alone party. As mentioned above, Lang describes Israelite religion during the period of the monarchy as a local variant of Near Eastern, Western Semitic polytheism:

> Each and every Israelite—from the King on down to the lowest slave— worshipped his own personal protective god, who had special relevance for health and family life. Yahweh was also worshipped as the national god, who had special responsibility for war and peace. Finally, all kinds of 'specialized gods' (*Ressortgötter*) were worshipped: these gods were responsible for all kinds of matters, such as weather and rain, the fertility of women, and such things.[42]

Yahweh's role in this context corresponds to that of other national gods, such as the Moabitic Chemosh, the Ammonite Milkom, the Assyrian Assur, or the Egyptian Amon-Re. Every nation had such a national god, who was a special object of worship in times of crisis and war, and in

all too often take their unquestioned point of departure in the Alt–Noth account of Israel's history and thus operate with a fictional contradiction between 'Canaanite' and 'genuine Israelite' religion. If we no longer can presume that the Israelites migrated to Palestine, but must suppose that Israelite society arose through an evolutionary process within what is 'Canaanite' (and if the amphictyony theory is dead), then the idea concerning the peculiarly 'Israelite' in Israel's religion must be abandoned. A careful consideration of this problem is to be found in Lemche, 'The Development of the Israelite Religion in Light of Recent Studies on the Early History of Israel'. It is, however, to be seen that Lemche's presentation in fact confirms the theory of Smith and Lang. He writes that 'It now looks as if the description of the Israelite religion in the formative period of the nation as a religion which contained a strictly monotheistic faith has to be surrendered...' (p. 17). This circumstance does not, however, invalidate Lemche's critique, but reveals on the contrary a lack of basic methodological consistency in the work of Smith and Lang.

41. Cf. his *Palestinian Parties and Politics that Shaped the Old Testament*, of which the second chapter (in German translation and with a new adaptation) makes up the first chapter of *Der einzige Gott*.

42. Lang, 'Die Jahwe-allein-Bewegung', pp. 53-54.

this respect Yahweh was no different from the other national gods. But faith in Yahweh, as over against belief in the other national gods, developed into a monotheistic religion with an emphasis on the demand for the exclusive worship of one all-embracing god. According to Lang, the reason for this difference is traceable to the fact that Yahweh, as opposed to the other national gods, was not a part of the local pantheon's familial system. The other gods had an organized relationship to one another, such as spouses, sisters, or children and parents. Yahweh was a loner, who stood outside the usual bonds. That is why a bitter strife could arise between Yahweh and Baal; the possibility for this is practically speaking to be found in Yahweh's very being. Another reason for the animosity can be found in the political and financial rivalry of the ninth century BCE between the adherents of the cult of Tyrean Baal, which was introduced by King Ahab and Queen Jezebel, who perhaps tried to make him into a national god in the Northern Kingdom, and the adherents of the national god Yahweh. Two national gods were one too many—'even the flexible logic of polytheism could not cope with that situation', as Lang puts it.[43]

Lang locates the beginning of the Yahweh-Alone Movement during the period of the turbulent political conditions that existed from the reign of Ahab (873–51) up to and including that of Jehu (843–16).[44] The oldest document from this movement is the book of Hosea.[45] We do not know how the Yahweh-Alone Movement developed in the century that lies between its beginnings and the time of Hosea, but one possibility is perhaps that the special worship of the national god mentioned above caused certain groups to practice 'temporary henotheism', as it is known from several places in the ancient Near East.[46] Such a form of henotheism, which in fact belongs to the polytheistic world picture, could during a period of the kind of crisis that existed in Northern Israel result in the idea of the permanent and exclusive worship of the national god. Yahwistic henotheism can thus be understood as a cult that arose during a crisis, a cult that continued after the crisis had passed.[47]

43. Lang, 'Die Jahwe-allein-Bewegung', p. 60.
44. The chronology is according to Miller and Hayes, *A History of Ancient Israel and Judah*, p. 220.
45. Lang, 'Die Jahwe-allein-Bewegung', p. 63.
46. Lang, 'Die Jahwe-allein-Bewegung', pp. 66ff. Lang refers to A. van Selms, 'Temporary Henotheism', pp. 34-48.
47. The understanding referred to may be seen as a continuation of the thought of

Summary and Conclusion

With this background material in mind, we must reject the idea that Hosea was a *restoration prophet*, who, in a cooperative effort with *orthodox* circles, wished to restore the cult to its *original monotheistic* source. That he himself understood it in this fashion or that he wished to represent the matter in this way is another issue. But from a historical point of view, it is far more probable that Hosea was a *reformer of the cult*. Hosea gave a new twist or emphasis to the traditions that he drew upon, traditions that were known to both the people and the priests. The dogma that Yahweh was Israel's God from the time in Egypt receives significance from the idea that Yahweh has a legal claim upon his people. And when Yahweh is placed within an agricultural context, as is the case in 10.11-13a, it must then be said that something utterly new is being said about this national god. But for Yahweh-Alone theology it becomes important to underscore that Yahweh so to speak embraces all the areas of life.[48]

This 'reallocation' of Yahweh comes most clearly to expression in the lawsuit against the faithless mother in 2.4-17. She believed that it was Baal that was the god of fertility. But he is not, says Hosea; in reality it is Yahweh. The people have forgotten that fact: that is the apostasy. This statement seems somewhat disingenuous.

Hvidberg in *Weeping and Laughter*, to which reference was made in the exegetical analysis (pp. 84-85, above), although neither Lang nor Smith makes mention of it. There is, however, a decisive difference in the approach to the material between Hvidberg and Smith–Lang, in that Hvidberg reckons with the existence of a 'pure' Yahweh cult as being incompatible with the cult of Baal, whereas Smith–Lang see the original Yahweh cult as an integrated part of 'Canaanite' religion. Lang has recently described Israel's religious milieu as a hierarchy consisting of four types of religion: (1) personal and family religion; (2) local religion; (3) national religion; (4) universal religion ('The Local God: Recognizing an Elementary Form of Ancient Israelite Religion', Lecture held at Aarhus University, March, 1990, unpublished manuscript, pp. 15-18). The theme of the popular cult on the high places is described by Balz-Cochois from the point of view of the participants, *Gomer*, pp. 95-187.

48. Lang mentions in this regard the identification that occurred between the national god Yahweh and the creator god El: cf. Gen. 2.7, where the name Yahweh is read into the older El story. And cf. Amos 9.6, with the addition 'Yahweh is his name' ('Die Jahwe-allein-Bewegung', pp. 55-56). Is this the same tendency that manifests itself in Exod. 6.3, where Yahweh identifies himself as *El Shaddai*?

Chapter 5

TRADITION AND PROPHECY—AN OVERVIEW

We have now reached the point where we can discuss the more general questions concerning the significance of the latter prophets (the writing prophets) for the development of Yahweh faith.

It has been a presupposition in what has preceded that the book of Hosea is the earliest reliable written witness we have in the Old Testament of the traditions concerning Israel's past. Another presupposition is to be added to this one, namely that the book of Hosea is one of the earliest documents we have of a henotheistic Yahweh religiosity.

This henotheism came more and more to the fore during the following centuries, eventually in the post-exilic period developing into the monotheism that is characteristic for Judaism. It is the essential presupposition for the great literary works of the Old Testament: the Tetrateuch, the Deuteronomistic History and the Chronicler's history. I have previously—albeit sporadically—touched upon the issue of how recent research understands their formation, and I will not say more about this matter here.

I will, however, in what follows provide a brief overview of the use of a motif that is known from the book of Hosea by some of the later prophets. This will be done partly by means of a presentation of the place of the finding and harmony motifs first in the book of Hosea itself and then in the books of Jeremiah and Ezekiel along with the closely related Song of Moses in Deuteronomy 32 and partly by indicating in what direction the present investigation of the Hosea tradition can be continued.

A. *Election, Exodus, and Finding in the Book of Hosea*

Robert Bach's Theory of the Finding and its Reception
In the preceding chapters I have occasionally made reference to Robert Bach's dissertation from 1952, 'Die Erwählung Israels in der Wüste'

('The Election of Israel in the Wilderness'). Although never published, it has since its appearance been a springboard for a large measure of the debate about Hosea's understanding of Israel's past. This is first and foremost due to the fact that both H.W. Wolff and W. Rudolph discuss Bach's dissertation in their commentaries: Wolff agrees with Bach's thesis while Rudolph rejects it.

Bach's theories have in many ways been rendered obsolete by the research done during the past 40 years. His secular historical assumptions are found in Martin Noth's *Geschichte Israels*, while his tradition-history point of view is dependent on Noth's *Überlieferungsgeschichte der Pentateuch*. The results of recent research have rendered it impossible to agree uncritically with the assumptions of Noth's work; but Bach's observation of a special variant of Election Theology in, among other places, the book of Hosea, still deserves to be taken into consideration in the exegetical debate. In what follows, I shall attempt to make a contribution in this regard.

Robert Bach's Theories

Two themes from the period in the wilderness have grown together in the Pentateuch, the theme of Yahweh's gracious guidance of the people and—contrapuntally—the reports of the people's 'murmuring' in the wilderness, which, all things considered, presents a rather negative picture of the earliest period. But the Old Testament also contains a positive evaluation of the attitude of the people in the wilderness, a tradition that comes through as a positive contrast to the theme of the 'people's murmuring'.

Bach undertakes a tradition-historical investigation of a number of Old Testament texts that have one common denominator, namely: 'Yahweh found Israel at the very outset in the wilderness'.[1] The point of departure is naturally the verb מצא (to find), Hos. 9.10aα, with which 'the beginning of the relationship between God and the people' is designated. ראה (to see), 9, 10aβ is interpreted in a parallel fashion as having the meaning 'catch sight of, become aware of' (p. 17). Hos. 10.11 is also understood in this regard as an expression for this beginning in the wilderness; עברתי (passing by) is viewed as a further parallel, which also contains traces of the idea of harmony between God and people: Yahweh

---

1. The texts are: Hos. 9.10; 10.11; Deut. 32.10; Ezek. 16.114; Hos. 2.5; 13.5; cf. 'Erwählung', p. 39.

'discovered them, found them to be useful, and took them into his service' (p. 21).[2]

This tradition can be designated as an *election tradition*. Different texts display different features of this tradition: Israel is identified as a *single individual*, a *person*. The people's earliest period is described as 'the period of her youth'. The reason for the election is the *worth* of the find. A *marriage* takes place between Yahweh and the people. Yahweh found Israel *in the wilderness* (p. 40).

In parallel fashion another tradition—or perhaps better, another theme—shows up in the idea that during the period in the wilderness utter harmony reigned between Yahweh and the people. When the two traditions are compared in their various versions, it is then seen that there is a 'striking, organic connection' between them (p. 47). But whereas the tradition of the finding (in the wilderness)—albeit its manifestations in the Old Testament are weak, having been outdone by the Exodus tradition—gives the impression of an original, almost corporeal fulness, the impression given by the harmony theme remains pale and schematic, indeed shadowy. The connection between the two—the finding tradition and the harmony tradition—allows one to presume that the finding tradition is the body that casts the shadow of the harmony tradition. Or—without employing Bach's imagery—the harmony tradition is what is left after the onward march of the Exodus tradition made it impossible to present the election as a finding (p. 48).

Bach picks up the scent of the finding tradition via the harmony tradition. As opposed to the Pentateuch, both the books of Hosea (2.16-17) and Jeremiah (2.2-3; 3.4-5a) represent the wilderness period as an ideal period, but without there being any 'nomadic ideal'.[3] In contrast to the prevalent view, according to which Jeremiah is understood to have been influenced by the book of Hosea, Bach argues that the two prophets independently of each other draw upon the same tradition about harmony, which they have found in the popular understanding of the matter. According to this view, the period in the wilderness is the time of the election. The harmony tradition is an expression of an awareness of election, and an awareness that since the election is based upon the idea that Yahweh found Israel to be especially valuable, then it is certain that Yahweh will continue to preserve his people (p. 12).

---

2.   See in addition Chapter 3 above.
3.   See especially the appendix to the monograph: 'Hos. 2,16-17 und das nomadische Ideal', pp. 50-58.

This popular understanding of the situation is used by the two prophets, each in his own way. Jeremiah is in agreement with the harmony tradition's account of the past (cf. also 2.5-8, 20; 6.16) and therefore contradicts the Pentateuchal tradition. But in opposition to the people's perception, he claims that 'the normal period in the wilderness' does not obligate Yahweh to 'further goodwill', but on the contrary admonishes the people to continued faithfulness (pp. 10ff.). For Hosea, on the other hand, the period that receives a positive evaluation is not the period in the wilderness, but the Exodus from Egypt. The harmony tradition is employed by Hosea as a model for a future ideal period.

Moreover, the fact that both Hosea and Jeremiah make use of marital terminology does not mean that Jeremiah is dependent upon Hosea. It could perhaps be supposed that this image was an integrated part of the harmony tradition, but after an investigation of Hos. 9.10, where the image is not found, this possibility is rejected. The marital terminology controls—both in the books of Hosea and Jeremiah—the complex into which the harmony tradition has been incorporated, and the marital picture is easily explained as having its basis in the popular religiosity of the time (pp. 15-16).[4]

The finding tradition is thus a popular election tradition, which in its present form stands in the shadow of the Exodus tradition. In the book of Hosea, Ezekiel 16, and Deuteronomy 32 the finding tradition appears precisely as a portion of or as an alternate presentation of this overarching tradition. But as we already have seen, its original theology was of another kind. To the question: 'How did it come about that Israel is the people of God, and Yahweh is the God of Israel?', it answers: 'When Yahweh once was going through the desert, he found Israel, recognized her value, and made her his possession'. Two things separate this tradition from that of the Exodus: (1) Israel's intrinsic value, which

---

4. A comment must be added to the above remarks. It is difficult to see the great difference between Jeremiah's and Hosea's use of the harmony tradition that Bach employs to support the idea that they had a common source in a popular conception. On the contrary, there is rather close agreement between the presentation and the idea of election in their thought, just as it must also be noted that Jeremiah in the same way as Hosea connects the period in the wilderness to the Exodus (Jer. 2.6) and later sees the apostasy as having taken place in the cultivated land (v. 7). All things considered, Bach does not succeed in convincing us that Jeremiah has not 'read' Hosea; thus, most recently, Carroll, *Jeremiah*, p. 119: 'The language and images may reflect the influence of the Hosea tradition (cf. Hos. 2.15; 9.10; 13.4-5; Deut. 32.10-14)'. See below, pp. 127-30.

was the occasion of Yahweh's action, as opposed to the Pentateuch's understanding of Yahweh's free, gracious act; (2) the emphasis on the idea that the place of this action was the desert. In this connection, Bach considers the possibility that the tradition of the finding could presuppose a different exodus tradition that establishes another place for the election than that of the Exodus from Egypt, specifically the place where the covenant at Sinai was ratified. But this possibility is rejected with reference to the fact that the Sinai pericope became a part—as a 'foreign body'—of the collected Pentateuchal tradition at a relatively late date. Indeed, the finding tradition knows nothing whatsoever about a sojourn in or an exodus out of Egypt (pp. 40ff.).

As to the origin of the finding tradition, Bach concludes (pp. 43-45) that its historical place of origin can in principle be found among all of the Israelite tribes that were not in Egypt. At the earliest it may have preceded the amphictyony with its Exodus and Covenant ratification theologies, perhaps deeply rooted in the cult. The mechanism by which it may have been passed on (and we are here dealing with a period of time that covers around 500 years without literary sources) is quite uncertain; but Bach mentions as a possibility a non-amphictyonic framework, in that he underscores the conservative nature of oral tradition and moreover makes a comparison with the Old Testament's third election tradition, the patriarchal narratives. But as opposed to these traditions, which were taken over by the cult of the covenant[5] and thus were made 'acceptable', the finding tradition was eliminated by amphictyonic censorship. We now find it only as a 'reverberation'.[6]

The Reception of the Theory of the Finding Tradition
The reactions to the finding theory in the scholarly world range from

---

5. Bach refers here to von Rad, *Das formgeschichtliche Problem des Hexateuchs*, and Noth, *Überlieferungsgeschichte des Pentateuch.*

6. Bach's interpretation of Deut. 32 and Ezek. 16 has not been mentioned in what precedes. *Deut. 32.10* is understood by Bach—in spite of the fact that the context is a product of the Exile—as being tradition-historically independent. The value of the foundling is not expressed *expressis verbis*, but Bach believes, nonetheless, that it is not contradicted (pp. 26ff.). In *Ezek. 16* Bach detects an original fairy tale, which refers back to the finding tradition (vv. 1-4), or rather, the finding tradition has attracted the fairy tale about the foundling. The fairy tale speaks of the foundling's beauty; it is first the prophet's 'inversion' of the original story with regard to Israel's apostasy that introduces the king's (Yahweh's) free grace (pp. 30ff). See further below, pp. 130-37.

absolute agreement to total rejection, *via* a partial acceptance of the theory along with a revision of it.

We find absolute agreement with Bach's theory in the work of H.W. Wolff,[7] who regards the finding theory with its special material outside of the Pentateuchal tradition as supporting his idea that Hosea belonged to esoteric circles that had their own body of tradition.[8] G. von Rad and G. Emmerson[9] are in agreement with the theory but do not expand upon it.

Total rejection is found in the work of W. Rudolph, who comments upon the theory at a number of points in the course of his commentary. While Hos. 9.10 (and 2.16-17) do indeed designate the period in the wilderness as 'the time of first love' (cf. Jer. 2.2), the verbs ראה, מצא and עבר (Hos. 10.11) do not give expression to an election theology. The idea that Israel should have had any independent value is a misunderstanding, an idea that both is fatal and that is utterly opposed to Hosea's convictions.[10]

While Rudolph's arguments are exegetical and theological by nature, those of C. Barth are tradition-critical. In a confrontation with the idea that the wilderness tradition has been subjected to transformations consisting of sharp 'breaks' in the tradition[11] (from an early portrayal of Yahweh's pure acts of salvation, via the view of the wilderness period as an ideal period, to the monarchical period's negative accentuation of the total rejection), Barth explicitly rejects Bach's idea that there has been any question of a positive understanding of Israel during the period in the wilderness in the above mentioned 'middle period'. In the places mentioned, the accent does not lie on Israel's attitude, but on the contrary on Yahweh's utterly gratuitous benefactions. Jer. 2.2 does not intend to point out Israel's actions but contrasts her apostasy with Yahweh's guidance. The wilderness period does not have any intrinsic interest for Hosea and Jeremiah. It is simply employed as a prelude to Israel's history; and the positive evaluation that Bach believes he finds

---

7. Wolff, *Hosea*, pp. 164, 185.

8. See Wolff, 'Hoseas geistige Heimat', and Chapter 4, pp. 101-107 above.

9. Von Rad, *Deuteronomium*, pp. 140-41, and cf. *Theologie des Alten Testaments*, I, p. 295; Emmerson, *Hosea*, p. 99.

10. Rudolph, *Hosea*, pp. 185, 202.

11. C. Barth, 'Zur Bedeutung der Wüstentradition'; for the finding tradition, see especially pp. 17-20.

among the prophets is an argument *e silentio*.[12]

A mediating position is taken by H. Gese. In an article on the history of the Sinai traditions he deals with Bach's theory about a special finding tradition, which he investigates and revises.[13] His presupposition is that the Sinai tradition is older than the Exodus tradition, and that it received a number of different reinterpretations through the passage of time. The Sinai tradition itself, therefore, is the point of departure for a finding tradition.[14] According to Gese, the three most important characteristics of the finding tradition have the Sinai tradition as a model: (1) the indication of the locality 'in the wilderness'; (2) that Yahweh meets Israel;[15] and (3) that Israel stands in an ideal relationship to Yahweh.[16]

The finding tradition is not, therefore (as opposed to Bach's understanding of the situation), ancient, but it presupposes a long period of living in the cultivated land. The disrupted relationship to Yahweh is the reason for looking back to the ideal primeval period, the history of salvation is the presupposition for the finding tradition, and the ideal period can be defined as the period in the wilderness *from* the Exodus. In this way the problem that the Exodus traditions and the finding traditions appear together in several places (Hos. 2.16-17; 11.1; 13.4, for example) is resolved.

The Sinai tradition undergoes a metamorphosis along with the finding tradition: a clear reference to the theophany and the concluding of the covenant on Sinai is missing. Instead of Yahweh's revelation, we have pictures of Yahweh's self-disclosure ('personale Selbsterschliessung'). Instead of a theophany, we learn that Yahweh sees, finds, knows and comes by. Marital, nuptial and child relationships appear in place of a real covenant. In other words: 'Instead of a place, the wilderness in general appears as Israel's primeval stage, and the revelatory event

12. For a skeptical point of view concerning the correctness of Bach's theory, see also Jeremias, *Hosea*, pp. 121-22, and Mays, *Hosea*, p. 133.

13. Gese, 'Bemerkungen zur Sinaitradition', pp. 40ff.

14. As opposed to Bach, whom Gese explicitly contradicts.

15. Gese notes that this meeting in the relevant texts is depicted by the use of varying expressions (מצא, ראה, נראה, עבר, ידע), which is why one ought not to speak onesidedly about a 'finding'-tradition. Some of the expressions (ידע, נראה and especially עבר) refer directly to the Sinai revelation (cf. Exod. 33.19-20; 1 Kgs 19.11) ('Bemerkungen zur Sinaitradition', pp. 41-42).

16. This is described as a fervent, intimate relationship (bride, child, son) and in this way the ideal excludes any idea concerning faithlessness and apostasy ('Bemerkungen zur Sinaitradition', p. 42).

becomes spiritualized into an intimate personal relationship' (pp. 42-43).

Gese finds a corresponding transformation in the original core of Deuteronomy,[17] which does not know anything about a covenant on Sinai or at Horeb, but only about a Moabite covenant. It is first during the reshaping of the material after the disaster in 587 that the old traditions about the events at Sinai and Horeb and the period in the wilderness are reincorporated.[18]

R. Kümpel also accepts the existence of a special tradition and tests the finding tradition against other מצא-material.[19] With a point of departure in Genesis 16, he finds, with regard to the report about how Yahweh's angel finds Hagar and Isaac at Beer-lahai-roi, that it is a question about 'an old Ishmaelite tribal tradition with its own theological program'.[20]

Summary

The questions that must subsequently be raised are as follows: can one speak at all about an independent *finding* tradition, or is the finding in the desert simply a motif that shows up again in a number of passages? Can we speak about an ideal period in the wilderness (harmony tradition)? Should a potential finding tradition be regarded as an election tradition? Can it—in agreement with Gese—be dependent upon the Sinai traditions (or, in agreement with Kümpel, can it be Ishmaelite)? How is the finding employed in different texts in and outside of the book of Hosea? And, in this connection, is there a literary and/or theological dependence between the individual authors, or is each one of them building independently on the tradition? Could the similarities possibly be utterly coincidental? And finally, what is the possible relationship between the finding tradition and the Exodus tradition?

The response to these questions takes its point of departure in the exegesis of the preceding chapters. From a literary/historical point of view, the book of Hosea provides the earliest evidence of the postulated

---

17. To this he assigns Deut. 6.4-9.6; 10.12–11.1; 27–28, 68. This primeval-Deuteronomy belongs in a theological historical sense together with Hosea, Jeremiah and the Song of Moses (Deut. 32) ('Bemerkungen zur Sinaitradition', pp. 44-43).

18. Neef, after a thorough analysis of the text, finds that 'Gese's understanding…is the most convincing position with regard to the texts investigated above' (*Heilstraditionen*, p. 117).

19. Kümpel, *Die Berufung Israels*, pp. 18-32.

20. Kümpel, *Die Berufung Israels*, p. 31.

finding tradition, and it must therefore—against Bach's perception of the situation[21]—be the point of departure for an investigation of this tradition.

Finding or No Finding?

Analysis

H.-D. Neef summarizes[22] Hosea's version of the tradition concerning Israel's election as follows:

> For Hosea the wilderness is the place where Israel's relationship to Yahweh was still intact, for there she had to rely completely on Yahweh's affection and help. He had chosen the people in the wilderness and had seen to it that the people had enough to eat (Hos. 13.5-6). Israel responded at first to this election and care with great thanksgiving (Hos. 9.10a; 10.1a, 11-12; 11.1a). With the entry into the cultivated land, however, the people increasingly turned away from their God and were more and more attracted to the temptations of the Canaanite Baal divinities (Hos. 9.10b; 10.1b; 11.2; 13.6). For this reason Hosea proclaimed Yahweh's judgment to his audience. The people must be made to leave the cultivated land behind and once again be led into the wilderness, so that they once again will be conscious of Yahweh's love and care and enter into a true renewal and deepening of their relationship to God. The second stay in the wilderness will therefore be a preliminary stage to a new occupation of the land and a hopeful life in peace with God and nature in the cultivated land (Hos. 2.16-25).[23]

In this summary the themes of the finding and of harmony are woven together into a complete presentation of Israel's (salvation-) history from the past into the future. In this way, there appears an inclusive, coherent and consistent picture of a theology of election. But is it really possible to find such a theology in the book of Hosea?

We have previously seen that Hosea regards Yahweh's election of Israel as the foundation for his claim upon the land and the people. We found in the book of Hosea a precursor to a covenantal theology, but without finding that it had decisive significance as a theologumenon, which it later received in the Deuteronomic/Deuteronomistic circle. Hosea finds an historical justification for Yahweh's demand for exclusivity. But

---

21. Bach, 'Erwählung', pp. 2ff.
22. Neef's textual basis is: Hos. 9.10-17; 10.1-2; 10.11-13a; 11.1-7; 13.4-8; 2.16-17; 12.10 (*Heilstraditionen*, p. 58 n. 1). He thus expands Bach's textual basis; see above, p. 117 n. 1.
23. Neef, *Heilstraditionen*, p. 58.

it is not possible to find support for the above cited paraphrase. When Neef claims that 11.1-7 deals with the period in the wilderness,[24] in spite of the clear speech about a call from Egypt (ממצרים קראתי לבני, 11.1b), it is clearly a case of harmonization. Yahweh's election is described in different ways according to the theme that Hosea is speaking of. There is thus to be found, as we have seen in Chapter 3, not only an election in the wilderness, but also in Egypt (11.1; 12.10; 13.4) and in the cultivated land (10.11-13a). The fact that Yahweh has chosen Israel is presented in different kinds of garb.[25]

The corresponding situation is evident if we limit our range of vision to the election in the wilderness. It can be described in such a way that Yahweh *finds* the people (מצא, 9.10), but also with the expressions that Yahweh *sees* them (ראה, 9.10, 13) and that he *gets to know them* (ידע, 13.5). It is therefore not advisable to speak about a special finding tradition. The fact that such a tradition was later reused (see p. 120 n. 6 and below, Section B) does not mean that it was a genuine tradition.

This understanding of the situation is strengthened, moreover, if we allow the diversity of the passages that deal with election to come to the fore. This can be seen below in the grouping of the different components of the election pericopes.

A. *The kind of election*:

finding	9.10a
seeing/getting to know	9.10aα, 13; 13.5 (10.11b)
calling	11.1

C. *The place of election*:

Egypt	11.1; 12.10; 13.4; 2.17
The wilderness	9.10a; 13.5
The cultivated land	10.11

---

24. Neef, *Heilstraditionen*, p. 114.

25. Yet another reservation must be made with regard to Neef's position, namely, that Hos. 10.1 ought not to be taken into consideration for the reason that the verse does not deal with election, but has election as its presupposition. There is indeed talk of a past, but not of a past in the wilderness. The verse describes the relationship after the settlement in the same way as 2.10–11.14. Israel is described as the fruitful, cultivated land, for, it is to be noted, the appellative Israel at the same time depicts both the land and its inhabitants. The land is fruitful, the inhabitants are fruitful, and things go well for them; but the better things go for them, the greater is the apostasy, that is, the more intensely they worship at the alters of idols and at the pillars. It is important here to be aware of the fact that the apostasy is not described as a break that occurred at the time of the settlement, but as a development *after* it.

C. *The relationship between Israel and Yahweh*:

Israel has value	9.10, 13; 10.11
obedience/harmony	12.10b; 13.4 (2.17)
unmentioned	11.1;[26] 13.5

A corresponding situation makes itself evident for the second important Hosean *dictum* that Israel is *apostate*. The apostasy is described in the election pericopes as having taken place

in the wilderness	13.6
on the border of the cultivated land	9.10b (2.17)
in the cultivated land	10.13 (10.1)

In addition, there are 11.1, 12.10 and 13.4, where the apostasy is not mentioned but where it on the other hand is underscored by the context.[27] Neef's talk about 'the tradition of the election in the wilderness'[28] is thus contradicted by the book of Hosea itself. In addition, his and Bach's idea of 'the tradition' must be modified to the extent that the passages that deal with election in the book of Hosea must be seen as expressions of a free use and development of several motifs. It is not a question of a genuine tradition.

From this it naturally follows that it is also impossible to speak about a special harmony tradition with a point of departure in the book of Hosea. In this regard, it is also a problem that Bach apparently does not distinguish between the two motifs of Israel's value and the harmony between God and the people (often based on Israel's obedience). In this way, he creates a broader basis for a tradition than the material permits.

Summary
We thus have grounds for rejecting the existence of a genuine *finding tradition*. The *motif* of the finding is found to be one of many images of the election. The theme of harmony can be employed or omitted—which is the same situation that Bach correctly saw is the case with the marriage motif (see above, p. 118). In addition, on the basis of these observations both Gese's and Kümpel's understandings of the finding tradition as a conversion of other traditions are to be rejected.[29]

---

26. See above p. 59.

27. To 11.1, see above, pp. 58-61; to 12.10, pp. 46, 63-64; to 13.4ff., pp. 73-77.

28. Cf. Neef, *Heilstraditionen*, p. 58.

29. Accordingly, we can spare ourselves a review of the literary reasons for rejecting the views of Gese and Kümpel; cf. further Chapter 1.

The idea that *finding* is identical to *election* and the fact that Hosea describes this election in quite different ways is, on the other hand, confirmed once again. We shall now follow the Election Theology in the shape of the finding motif in later Old Testament books.

B. *The Motif of the Finding after the Book of Hosea*

Robert Bach regarded the finding and harmony 'traditions' in Jeremiah 2, Ezekiel 16 and Deuteronomy 32 as being independent of Hosea, based on a popular tradition that also lies behind the book of Hosea. But as already noted, Bach did not succeed in convincing us of the truth of his claims. Against Bach, but without taking special regard to his own views in the argument, we shall in what follows try to understand the passages mentioned as expressions of a continuous tradition.

Jeremiah 2.1-3

In Jer. 2.1-3, which is presumably the oldest instance of the finding motif after the book of Hosea, we find it in this form:

> 1 The word of Yahweh came to me:
> 2 Go and proclaim to Jerusalem:
> Thus says Yahweh:
> I remember the devotion of your youth,
> your love as a bride.
> You followed me in the wilderness, in a land not sown.
> 3 Israel was holy to Yahweh, the first fruits of his harvest.
> All who ate of it were held guilty,
> disaster came upon them,
> says Yahweh.

The introduction, 'The word of Yahweh came to me: Go and proclaim to Jerusalem', is an expansion of MT in relation to LXX, which here reflects an older text. The same is the case for the words 'in the wilderness, in a land not sown' (v. 2).[30] The original text thus had no conception of the wilderness, but appeared as follows:

> 2* Thus says Yahweh:
> I remember the devotion of your youth,
> your love as a bride.
> 3 Israel was holy to Yahweh, the first fruits of his harvest.
> All who ate of it were held guilty,
> disaster came upon them, says Yahweh.

30. Cf. *BHS a-a.b-b*; McKane, *Jeremiah*, I, p. 27.

Jer. 2.2-3 stands as the introduction to the poetic block, Jeremiah 2–6, whose themes have a close affinity with themes known from Hosea: Jer. 2.4–4.4, the apostasy of the people, depicted with the metaphor of whoring, and Jer. 4.5–6.26, the destruction from the North. The block concludes with an address to the prophet, who is installed as a tester of the people. We have here a collection of poetry, in which different redactions, Deuteronomistic as well as post-Deuteronomistic, have inserted prose commentary.[31] The block itself is a secondary collection, but on the whole it consists of material from Jeremiah. This is also the case for Jer. 2.2-3.[32]

The concept of finding is not present in Jer. 2.2-3. There is, however, clearly talk about harmony between the people and Yahweh in the very beginning. This beginning was not connected with a wilderness motif in the earliest form of the text, and the harmony between Yahweh and the people is therefore not defined as something that belongs to the wandering in the wilderness. This connection was first made at a later date. But the text intended to stress the *original* harmony, the happy primeval relationship between Yahweh and the people, which was the foundation for their later life together.

In this way the text is in agreement with ideas to be found in Hosea, which indeed also contains conceptions of the harmonious primeval period. But while the idea of harmony in the book of Jeremiah is, as we have seen, utterly devoid of an historical link,[33] in the book of Hosea it is historically defined as belonging to the election in Egypt (2.17b [MT]; 11.1). While we should not make too much of this fact, there seems to be here a difference between the two prophets. Since the wilderness motif is 'missing' in Jeremiah, it can be the case that it was unimportant in the original context.[34] What was important here was an emphasis on the almost mystical harmony. Jeremiah does not thus have a veritable

---

31. See further in this regard my own *Fra profeti til prædiken*, pp. 426-37. W. Thiel, *Die deuteronomistische Redaktion von Jeremia 1–25*, pp. 80ff., is somewhat skeptical with regard to Deuteronomistic influence on 3.6-18.

32. W. Schottroff regards Jer. 2.1-3 as having been formulated by the exilic redaction of the material with a view to 2.4-13 ('Jeremia 2,1-3: Erwägungen zur Methode der Prophetenexegese').

33. The lack of such has led to the clarifying addition in the MT, perhaps under the influence of the Hosean tradition.

34. This 'lack' would also seem to indicate that the text has been drawn up with regard to what follows, but contains a Jeremian core.

'dating' of the harmonic period,[35] but it is depicted as the time of youth and marriage. In this way Jeremiah is in complete agreement with, on the one hand, Hos. 2.17 (MT) and 11.1, and, on the other hand, with the betrothal metaphor in Hos. 2.21-22 (MT).

We do, therefore, find the harmony idea in Jeremiah,[36] but at the same time the passage bears witness to the fact that this idea belongs to a later period, the exilic and post-exilic period.

The harmony idea is placed before an exposition of the people's apostasy, and in this way it stands clearly as a contrast that places the present situation in relief—but not only the present. It is evident from the following pericope (Jer. 2.4-9), which is the first in the section Jer. 2.2–4.4, that the apostasy began with the fathers, who came into possession of the land, that it has continued with the present generation, and that it will have consequences right up until the time of 'the sons of your sons'.[37] The idea in this pericope corresponds, therefore, rather well with what comes to expression in Hos. 9.10; 10.13; 10.1,[38] according to which the apostasy against Yahweh began with the settlement of the land and continued with increasing strength in the following period. The idea in Jer. 2.9 must be as follows: since idol worship has such great power over the people, it will continue unabated.

In the account of Israel's attitude towards Yahweh there is a description of Yahweh's guidance of the people in the wilderness. The murmuring of the people in the wilderness, which is a characteristic motif in the Pentateuch, does not appear. On the contrary, the historical *vue* of the guidance in the wilderness underscores the good relationship between God and the people, while, as opposed to Hosea, there is not in this context any talk about the intrinsic value of the people. The idea of election does not seem to be a basic feature in the presentation. Here again the situation is different from that in the book of Hosea. The

35. Neither is Israel ascribed any intrinsic worth in the book of Jeremiah. Israel is not referred to as 'beautiful' or 'fertile' (cf. Hos. 9.10; 10.1).

36. Carroll believes that Jer. 2.1-3 does not contain Jeremian material, and he interprets the entire pericope as the expression of a theology that is found in the final, post-LXX text, i.e., MT (*Jeremiah*, pp. 188ff.). It is more likely that we find in 2.2-3 a Jeremian core, which has been worked over at a later stage. See in this regard my *Fra profeti til prædiken*, pp. 242-45.

37. See Carroll, *Jeremiah*, p. 123.

38. The picture of Israel as a vine is also found in Jer. 2.21; Ps. 80.9, 15-16; cf. Isa. 5.1-10 and see in this connection K. Nielsen, *There is Hope for a Tree*, pp. 87-123.

picture here stands between, on the one hand, Hosea's rhetoric about Yahweh's guidance in the wilderness (which Jeremiah understands to be identical with election) and, on the other hand, that of the Pentateuch's, which (in any case in its final form) describes the election as a covenantal agreement and employs the period of the wandering in the wilderness as also being an illustration of Yahweh's goodness. The original harmony is therefore also emphasized in the pericope, without, however, there being any mention of the people's attitude.

Jeremiah thus employs the harmony motif, but not the finding motif.[39] It is a different story in the book of Ezekiel.

Ezekiel 16

According to W. Zimmerli,[40] Ezekiel 16, where the finding motif is played through, is a redactional unit, where the pericopes in vv. 44-58 and 59-63 must be, because of their theme, separated from what precedes, although they do resume key words from the previous section. These pericopes are without any significance for understanding Ezekiel's use of the tradition of the finding in the wilderness, in that they characterize a further development, that is, a 'later interpretation' (*Nachinterpretation*) of the tradition. We shall therefore focus our attention on the first part of the chapter.

In *Ezek. 16.1-43* we find the story of the 'foundling', Jerusalem, who was thrown out into the wilderness because of her mixed descent, but was found by Yahweh, who took care of her, that is, gave her life, and later, when she became an adult, married her (vv. 1-14). But she showed herself to be faithless, whored with others, and even sacrificed Yahweh's own children to foreigners (vv. 15-21). She forgot the days of her youth and whored with foreign nations, the Egyptians, the Assyrians and the Chaldeans, without even having received a 'decent' whore's wages. On the contrary, she was the one who purchased lovers (vv. 22-34). Therefore, Yahweh will now punish her by gathering her lovers together against her, and he will exhibit her for them, uncovered in her nakedness. They will destroy her platform, the place where she conducted her business, and they will plunder her, stone her, and burn her houses down (vv. 35-43).

---

39. The picture of the father–son/daughter relationship in Jer. 3.4.19 cannot be used to support the finding motif. It belongs thematically closer to Hos. 11.

40. The following takes its point of departure in W. Zimmerli, *Ezekiel*, I, pp. 331-71.

The finding motif is foundational in Ezekiel 16, where it receives a narrative expansion with what amounts to a nearly allegorical description of the conditions that pertained at the time of the 'illegitimate' child's birth.[41] The entity Israel, which, according to Zimmerli, Ezekiel has adopted via Jeremiah from the book of Hosea, is redefined as 'Jerusalem', and the background for and the circumstances surrounding the finding are meticulously depicted. When the child was born, none of the things that are usually done to nurture and keep a child alive were done.[42] No one wished that the child should live. But Yahweh found[43] the exposed child and gave it life, in that he, as is the case in the Priestly creation report, acts by means of his word. Command and blessing converge into one reality, and in the words 'you shall live' there is more to be found than mere physical life; here resound also happiness, vitality and nearness to God.[44] It would thus seem to be the case that the finding tradition in the book of Ezekiel in addition to being an election tradition (and that is beyond doubt) also receives the character of a kind of creation report. In this regard it is important to take note of how the people's return (through the wilderness) and creation merge in the slightly later Deutero-Isaiah (for example, Isa. 42.5-9; 43).

According to Zimmerli, a clear re-accentuation has taken place in relation to Hosea and Jeremiah. While these last two speak about 'the bright early period', where a *reciprocity* ruled between God and the people, Yahweh's efforts in the book of Ezekiel are placed in the larger perspective of the 'foundling's' sorry state.[45] It is thus not a question of

41. The presentation in v. 3 of Jerusalem's descent intends to specify this: the designations כנעני and אמרי have more than geographical significance, in that they refer back to the settlement traditions. In this connection it must be mentioned that Ezekiel is of course capable of playing upon the traditions of the settlement, without these necessarily being historical or ancient. One does not thus need to be in agreement with the 'classical' view of the Canaanites or of the occupation of the land in order to share Zimmerli's understanding. That the 'mother' is designated as a Hittite (חתית) can perhaps be due to Ezekiel's reliance on old traditions about Hittite influence in Jerusalem. See Zimmerli, *Ezekiel*, I, pp. 347-48.

42. Verses 4-5 are stylized like a creation report; see Zimmerli, *Ezekiel*, I, pp. 348-49, and below.

43. Note that the verb עבר is used. Compare Hos. 10.11, where עבר is used synonymously with מצא; see Bach, 'Erwählung', p. 21 and above, pp. 124-26.

44. Zimmerli, *Ezekiel*, I, pp. 348ff.

45. According to Zimmerli, Ezekiel here develops a motif, 'naked as on the day she was born', from Hos. 2.5. It is, however, not necessary to see such a dependence,

any conception of harmony or of the intrinsic value of the foundling. On the contrary, Jerusalem's utter unworthiness and helplessness are underscored.[46] Only Yahweh's actions are capable of giving her any value whatsoever. Even when she became sexually mature, no one was interested in caring for her. Yahweh married her and made her into the most beautiful queen, but she showed herself to be utterly unworthy of this honor.

In the description of the chosen one's faithlessness we are able to recognize a theme from Hosea, namely, that all good things come from Yahweh. But while the most significant accusation in Hosea (2.4-15 [MT]) is that these good things are perceived as gifts from Baal, the stress in Ezek. 16.15-21 is laid upon something else, namely that they were sacrificed to the foreign deities. The accusation of political 'whoring' is also a continuation of ideas in the book of Hosea. But also this part of the portrayal is substantially expanded in relation to the book of Hosea's more terse and at times merely intimating style. The foreign lovers are, in addition to those known to Hosea, namely the Egyptians and the Assyrians, also the Philistines (who apparently do not play any special role for Hosea) and the Chaldeans, who assumed major importance *after* the time of Hosea.[47]

What is the effect of this metaphorical language about Jerusalem's apostasy against Yahweh? Zimmerli refers to the phenomenon of *corporate personality*, which has been pointed out by H.W. Robinson,[48] according to which a group of people are presented as one particular person. It is in this way that figures of speech such as 'the daughter of Zion' (Jer. 4.31) or 'the daughter of Babylon' (Jer. 50.42) and thus here simply 'Jerusalem' are to be understood, in that groups or cities are

since what is interesting for Hosea is not so much the point in time for the nakedness as it is the kind of nakedness involved. Ezekiel, on the other hand, plays upon the idea that the child is more than naked, in that it has not been cared for.

46.   Bach believes that in an original fairy tale, that lies behind Ezek. 16, it was a question of the girl as 'the most beautiful girl in the world', i.e., of Israel's intrinsic worth. The emphasis on Yahweh's 'free grace' in Ezek. 16 stems therefore from the prophet himself (Bach, 'Erwählung', p. 33).

47.   In vv. 15-34, Zimmerli regards only vv. 15 and 24-25 as 'the basic component of the description of sin'. It is, however, also evident that the remainder of the presentation, which to some extent stems from Ezekiel's own 'pen', and to some extent is a 'later interpretation' (*Nachinterpretation*), has been inspired by Hosea's polemics against both cultic and political apostasy (*Ezekiel*, I, pp. 353ff.).

48.   H.W. Robinson, 'The Concept of Corporate Personality'.

often shown in the image of a woman. This practice is the background for Hosea's presentation of Israel as a whore (Hos. 1.2; 2.4-15 [MT]), which is later taken over by Isaiah (1.21), Jeremiah (3), and Ezekiel. As Zimmerli puts it, the language about Jerusalem as the faithless woman is:

> more than a freely chosen allegorical pictorial covering made on the basis of purely aesthetic considerations. The reality of the people lives within this image. In Ezek. 16 (and 23) the distance between imagery and substance is thus suddenly capable of being cancelled, and what is meant stands out clearly in the metaphorical language employed. The reality is not only artistically represented. It is present with its uncanny power in the image itself.[49]

This understanding is supported by the definition of Old Testament metaphorical language that Kirsten Nielsen sets forth in her monograph, *There is Hope for a Tree.* Among other things, this definition includes the idea that metaphors have *informative* and *performative* functions.[50] With regard to the matter at hand, this definition shows that the point of Ezekiel's metaphorical speech was that the audience should be able to identify itself with the shameless, faithless woman and that they should be able to understand their situation after they have been punished.[51] In

49. Zimmerli, *Ezekiel,* I, p. 34.
50. Nielsen, *There is Hope for a Tree,* pp. 65-66; see further her conclusions, pp. 223-39.
51. Thus also F. van Dijk-Hemmes deals with the use of feminine metaphors in Ezek. 23 in an unpublished short communication at the IOSOT Congress in Leuven in August 1989 ('The Metaphorization of Woman in Prophetic Speech: An Analysis of Ezekiel 23'). Her perception that the condemnation was especially directed towards the female members of the prophet's audience must be rejected precisely because of the common usage of female metaphors for cities (see above, p. 132). It thus seems incomprehensible that van Dijk-Hemmes, having laid emphasis on the idea that it was especially humiliating for the masculine members of the audience to hear themselves compared with a woman, should underscore that it is precisely the metaphor's 'androcentric-pornographic character which at the same time offers the male audience a possibility of escape: the escape of an identification with the revengeful husband', whereas this possibility is not open for the female members of the audience. The latter would only have been able to hear Ezek. 23—and the same must be the case for Ezek. 16—as 'a violent speech act which, at the same time, shapes and distorts her (sexual) experience' (p. 9). One could indeed ask which female members of the audience van Dijk-Hemmes includes in her understanding of the situation, but more important is the fact that one of the successful metaphor's characteristics is that it is *performative* and thus does not leave the listener any real possibility for getting off the hook, not even if the metaphor is unpleasant to hear. I owe the late F. van Dijk-Hemmes a word

order to achieve this goal, Ezekiel has given the motif a previously unknown expansion.

It is therefore not the case that Ezekiel has taken over a previously known narrative entity, an adventure, or a tradition.[52] What he has taken over is the tradition itself that Yahweh found Israel in the wilderness. The rest he did 'on his own'.

Deuteronomy 32

The last occurrence of the finding motif that will be discussed is Deut. 32.10-18. The context, the so-called 'Song of Moses', is a late- or post-exilic composition.[53] The prophetic *rîb-pattern* is regarded by many as being constitutive for the form of the poem,[54] but its use in Deuteronomy 32 is far removed from the original *Sitz im Leben*. The form has been expanded and reworked with a view to a completely different purpose. The influence of wisdom literature on the poem is quite comprehensive.[55] There is also an obvious affinity with Hosean thinking.[56]

of thanks for having graciously provided me with a copy of her manuscript. I also want to thank Professor Kirsten Nielsen for having called my attention to its existence.

52. Against Bach, 'Erwählung', p. 32: 'If Israel already before Ezekiel had not been the object of the story about the foundling, then the adoption of this story for the use by the prophet for a presentation of the history of Jerusalem would be utterly incomprehensible'.

53. 'The song of Moses and the Blessing of Moses with their introductions are post-deuteronomistic additions, [...], since the Deuteronomistic context clearly does not presuppose their presence. The Song is probably as late in composition as the time of its insertion here...' (Mayes, *Deuteronomy*, p. 372). And cf. Hidal, 'Reflections on Deuteronomy 32', p. 19. 'The song of Moses' has moreover been dated to almost every conceivable period, from the eleventh century (Eissfeldt) to the Persian period (R. Meyer).

54. For example, G.E. Wright, 'The Lawsuit of God. A Form Critical Study of Deuteronomy 32'. On the basis of his form-critical observations, Wright believes that the Song of Moses ought to be dated to the eleventh century with the Philistines' conquest of Israel, the destruction of the central shrine at Shilo, and the abduction of the ark (p. 66).

55. Von Rad, *Deuteronomium*, 140; Mayes, *Deuteronomy*, pp. 280-81.

56. In addition to the connection between Deut. 32.10 and the finding tradition in the book of Hosea, compare Deut. 32.15 and Hos. 2.4-9; 9.10; 13.1-2 (see E. Nielsen, 'Historical Perspectives and Geographical Horizons', n. 27) and the line of reasoning in Deut. 32.39 and Hos. 6.1-3.

The structure of the poem reflects the (post-)Deuteronomistic understanding of Israel's relationship to Yahweh: after the so-called 'summons to hear' (*Lehreröffnungsruf*)[57] and an exhortation to honor the God who has created his 'foolish and senseless people', there follows a presentation of Yahweh's history with Israel (vv. 8-18). This is then followed by a judgment speech (vv. 19-25), which, however, is immediately modified by Yahweh's considerations in the form of a monologue (*Selbstgespräch*)[58] concerning the idea that the enemies will misinterpret the destruction of the people as an expression of weakness on Yahweh's part (vv. 26-30). Yahweh will obtain justice for his people, the gods of the nations are nothing, and Yahweh is the one, true God (vv. 31-42). A climax that reveals the major message of the poem is reached in v. 39.[59] The poem concludes with a hymnic strophe (v. 43).

The message thus bears to some degree the stamp of Deuteronomistic influence, but the Deuteronomistic judgment theology in the post-Deuteronomist era has been modified by rather clear indications that Yahweh will now desist from punishing his sinful people, not so much for the sake of the people, but in order that it can be seen that he is the only, invincible God.[60]

We discover the finding motif in the part of the poem that deals with Israel's history in relation to Yahweh, which begins as follows:

> He sustained him in a desert land,
> in a howling wilderness waste;
> he shielded him, cared for him,
> guarded him as the apple of his eye (Deut. 32.10).

Yahweh is described as an eagle and a rock, Israel (here called Jeshurun[61]) as an overly spoiled domestic animal. As was the case in the book of Hosea, the motif is used to underline the seriousness of Israel's apostasy and its opposite, Yahweh's care.[62] This theme is the mainstay of

---

57. Von Rad, *Deuteronomium*, p. 139.
58. Von Rad, *Deuteronomium*, p. 142.
59. See now that I, even I, am he;
    there is no god beside me.
  I kill and I make alive;
    I wound and I heal;
    and no one can deliver from my hand.
60. We also find the idea of a softening of the punishment in the Deuteronomistic reworking of the book of Jeremiah.
61. Cf. Deut. 33.5, 26; Isa. 44.2.

the entire presentation in vv. 10-14.

Some scholars are astonished that the historical presentation in Deuteronomy 32 does not include the events at Sinai. The poem underscores Yahweh's demand for exclusivity, but this claim is based on election, not on a covenantal agreement. When one considers the weight that is laid upon the covenant both during and after the Deuteronomic movement, it is then natural to reflect upon why the poem's 'author'[63] has placed the emphasis on this other aspect.

But the Sinai covenant does not belong in this context, just as it is not mentioned in other historical enumerations, as, for example, the historical credo in Deut. 26.5-9. As holds true for the book of Hosea, it is the finding motif that denotes the election. In this connection it is important to take into consideration that we are indeed here dealing with a pure Deuteronomistic product. There are also found echoes of Deutero- and Trito-Isaianic language and thinking, just as there also can be observed a certain affinity with the exposition of the history of salvation that we find in Nehemiah 9.[64]

In contrast to the book of Hosea, we do not find in Deut. 32.10 any hint of a harmonious relationship between Yahweh and Israel or any mention of the intrinsic worth of the foundling. Deut. 32.10 simply underscores Israel's helpless situation. This corresponds to what we found in the book of Ezekiel. But the book of Ezekiel's account moreover seems to have been without influence on Deut. 32.10. One can, therefore, cautiously conclude that the presence of the finding motif in Deuteronomy 32 is not to be explained by its use in the book of

---

62. Mayes does not believe that the emphasis lies on a reproduction of the finding motif, but precisely on its use (*Deuteronomy*, p. 385). But this does not, of course, differentiate Deut. 32.10 from the other passages where we have found the motif.

63. The word 'author' conceals here the fact that the different traditions are freely used with a definite main point in mind. Form-critical investigations of Deut. 32 show that it is meaningless to attempt to divide the poem up into different literary sources. See, for example, already E. Baumann, 'Das Lied Moses (Dt. XXXII 1-43) auf seine gedankliche Geschlossenheit untersucht', against P. Winther, 'Der Begriff "Söhne Gottes" im Moselied Dt. 32,1-43', who, on the basis of the term 'the sons of God', divides Deut. 32 up into two sources, an older and a younger 'song' (p. 45).

64. Hidal, 'Reflections on Deuteronomy 32', p. 19. The poem's originality over against the theological 'main schools' is also underscored, for example, by Noth, who regards the poem as one of the latest additions to Deuteronomy (*Überlieferungsgeschichtliche Studien*, p. 40).

Ezekiel, but, conversely, that the motif has probably been borrowed from Hosea. We also found such borrowing in the book of Jeremiah, only there it was not the finding motif but the harmony motif that was put to use. We have thus yet again found support for arguing that the two motifs are not inextricably bound together. Only that motif has been employed which fits in with the matter being discussed. For this reason it is also legitimate to pose the question whether the same circles stand behind Jeremiah 2 and Deuteronomy 32.[65]

E. Nielsen argues for a Northern origin and a pre-exilic dating of the poem, precisely because of its affinity with the book of Hosea.[66] The late stamp that has been placed upon the poem by the use of many different form elements and by the influence of Wisdom literature speaks against this idea. Deuteronomy 32 is indeed characterized by a piling up of images, a use of *mythologumena*, which according to S. Hidal 'have no independent theological function, but have been used to render the poem archaistic'.[67] Hidal places Deuteronomy 32 in the restoration milieu after the return from the Exile:

> At this time a wave of interest in more ancient times could be perceived throughout the entire Orient (Nabonidus), and it seems highly improbable that Israel was not affected. Deut. 32 and 33 express this interest. The author's efforts to create the correct atmosphere are impressive: the archaic language, the mythological elements and the ancient world of ideas (e.g. the 'finding-tradition' in v. 10).[68]

But these archaizing traits did not come out of nowhere,[69] and, considering the proximity of a number of features in the poem to Hosean material as a whole, it cannot be dismissed that the finding idea also stems from the book of Hosea, mediated by circles where prophetic theology was kept alive.[70]

65. The final editing of the book of Jeremiah presumably took place in the post-exilic period. See Carroll, *Jeremiah,* pp. 69ff.
66. Nielsen, 'Historical Perspectives and Geographical Horizons', p. 86.
67. Hidal, 'Reflections on Deuteronomy 32', p. 18.
68. Hidal, 'Reflections on Deuteronomy 32', pp. 18-19.
69. Concerning Deut. 32.8-9, Bach, 'Erwählung', p. 26, writes: 'An exilic or even a post-exilic writer would not make up something like this'. That Bach moreover rejects the intellectual content, in which the different traditions are made use of in the final poem, Deut. 32, is another matter, which is not under discussion here.
70. As previously mentioned, Bach regards also Deut. 32.10 and the finding traditions in the book of Hosea as an expression of the same tradition formation, but he believes that the two instances of the finding tradition are independent of each

C. *Other Theological Traces*

We have now followed the finding motif to 'the end of the road', and we can conclude that it has been a specifically vital motif. It lived side by side with the idea of the election by means of a covenantal agreement. It is therefore more proper to describe Israel's religion as an *election* religion rather then a *covenantal* religion, or, better, *the idea of the covenant is neither the only nor necessarily the most important theological expression of Israel's relationship to God in all areas of the Old Testament.*

This is perhaps a banal ascertainment on the basis of the Old Testament itself, but not if one takes as the point of departure the results of this century's Old Testament research. As known, it was Wellhausen's idea that the תורה was built upon prophecy; but after a certain amount of debate, this point of view was abandoned in favour of the understanding that the covenant was an ancient, inalienable and totally dominating factor in Israelite religion.[71] This understanding, which has been supported by the theory of the amphictyony, has been a paradigm for research until quite recently, in spite of the recent demise of the theory of the primitive amphictyony. And even for E.W. Nicholson, who (as, for example, Perlitt) regards the covenant as 'a theological innovation of a later time',[72] it turns out to be the case that even after closer inspection covenantal theology is the key to the question of 'the distinctiveness of Israel's religious faith'.[73]

It seems to me, however, to be plausible that one ought rather with Martin Rose to speak of Yahweh's demand for exclusivity as being decisive for understanding Israelite religion. When we turn to the Priestly theology, we can see that the covenant does not have the central significance that it obviously has for the Deuteronomists. And for the contemporaries of the Deuteronomists, Deutero-Isaiah and certain parts of the book of Jeremiah, we find the election grounded in utterly different

other. This is related to the fact that he regards Deut. 32 as having been made up of autonomous, ancient traditions, which have been placed together in untreated form ('Erwählung', pp. 26ff.).

71. For the history of covenantal research, see E.W. Nicholson, *God and his People*, chs. 1-4, which not only provide a review of the different points of view in the research, but also give the reader their societal background.

72. Nicholson, *God and his People*, p. 191.

73. Nicholson, *God and his People*, p. 191.

things than the Sinai or Horeb covenant: namely, in Yahweh's guidance of his people in the desert.

Is it here a question of an inheritance from the Hosean material? Do we hear, for example, Hosea's voice in Jeremiah's 'Book of Consolation', Jeremiah 30–31?[74] Much indicates that this is so, but the answer to the question presupposes rather thorough investigations of the ideological milieu in which Jeremiah's 'Book of Consolation' arose, as to whether it was in the exilic or the post-exilic period.[75] Such investigations do not belong here, but I hope that they can be set forth in a future publication.

Another area of research that the present investigations of the book of Hosea can provide a basis for is the tradition-historical connections between the book of Hosea and the Tetrateuch *in the order stated*, that is, the question as to whether the book of Hosea possibly can have had some influence on the final formation of the stories in the Tetrateuch. A late dating of the Tetrateuch opens up certain possibilities for these ideas, especially when it is borne in mind that we in this way get a much closer chronological connection between the use of the tradition of the finding in the books of Jeremiah and Ezekiel along with Deuteronomy 32 and the Yahwist's composition. This area also demands rather comprehensive investigations and perhaps even a new stage in the development of our research, which we have just begun to move towards within the past few years.

---

74. See S. Böhmer, *Heimkehr und neuer Bund*, where this connection is touched upon in connection with a discussion of the 'genuineness' of Jer. 30–31, which Böhmer believes to be a *corpus mixtum*.

75. See also further in this regard Carroll, *Jeremiah*, pp. 568-618.

Chapter 6

CONCLUSION

After this overview of the continued life of the Hosean traditions in the Old Testament, we now return to the book of Hosea itself, in that we must see what the consequences of the exegetical investigations in the preceding chapters mean for an understanding of the book's theology.

Two concepts have constantly made their presence felt in the course of these investigations, namely, Yahweh's demand for exclusivity and the knowledge of God, דעת אלהים. The point of departure for the understanding of דעת אלהים has been H.W. Wolff's understanding of the concept as a cognitive one as opposed to the more widespread understanding of the concept as an emotional category. The validity of this point of departure has been confirmed in the investigations. It was indeed demonstrated that the demand for דעת אלהים was a demand for something other than just an emotional relationship to Yahweh, even though it must be expressed in a human attitude, חסד.

חסד is in fact not an emotional concept. As previously mentioned, A. Jepsen has defined secular, interhuman חסד as 'good will, in so far as it manifests itself in good deeds'.[1] The emotional element is only valid to the extent that it makes itself known in actions. Jepsen rejects—presumably for dogmatic reasons—the idea that human beings are able to show forth חסד vis-à-vis God. But this rejection is clearly contradicted by the texts themselves; there is no categorical difference between interhuman חסד and the חסד that people direct towards God. Although it is not his intention to do so, Jepsen's definition can be employed in relation to Yahweh: חסד can be understood as the human response to Yahweh's action. Human beings receive knowledge about this action by experiencing דעת אלהים, which conversely may be understood as a presupposition for חסד. If one recognizes דעת אלהים, then the natural reaction is that one shows forth חסד. By this is not meant the 'pietistic' faith's fervour, that is, something emotional, but rather the actions that one can with

1. Jepsen, 'Gnade und Barmherzigkeit im Alten Testament', p. 269.

'fairness' expect of that person who has received Yahweh's gifts of salvation. Indeed, one could say that it is by showing חסד that one demonstrates that one has in fact received these gifts.

חסד ought, therefore, to be a consequence of דעת אלהים. What, then, is the content of this דעת? What is it that Israel must know? According to Wolff, it is the 'knowledge of Yahweh's acts of salvation and gifts of justice';[2] according to Zimmerli, 'the "divine right" of Israel'.[3] The knowledge of God is the knowledge about how he has obtained his rightful position vis-à-vis Israel, about how he has acted for Israel in history. He chose Jacob in Bethel, he called Israel out of Egypt and protected her, he found her in the desert, and he domesticated her and gave her what she needed for sustenance. In all of these actions it is clear that Yahweh has chosen Israel. Therefore Israel must show Yahweh חסד, or, in other words: therefore, Israel must submit herself to Yahweh's demand for exclusivity.

Yahweh's dealings with Israel in history are the content of דעת אלהים. It is the task of the priests to mediate this דעת in the cult, but they have failed in this task. Among other things, this is why, as Wolff also underscores,[4] Hosea occupies himself so intensely with Israel's prehistory precisely as a history with Yahweh. He does this in two different ways: by telling about exemplary figures and by recalling the events of Israel's history; and the knowledge of God that he will create has two different objectives: conversion and awareness.

In Chapter 2 we saw how Hosea tells his stories of Jacob by the use of key words and interprets the Jacob traditions as an exemplary story for Israel. Descendants of that Jacob, who tended cattle in a foreign country, were themselves led out of a foreign country and were tended by Yahweh's prophet (12.13-14). He, who deceived his brother and struggled with God, was chosen by Yahweh of Hosts in Bethel (12.4-5). It is no longer clear as to how much more Hosea and his audience knew about Jacob's escapades, or how much more there was to be known at all, that is, how many and which traditions about Jacob were in circulation in Hosea's age and surroundings. We have been able to conclude that, by the use of storytelling techniques, Hosea has abbreviated longer reports that can be assumed to have been familiar to the audience; but we are unable to draw any inferences from either the book of Hosea or

2.   Wolff, 'Wissen um Gott', p. 198.
3.   Zimmerli, 'Gottesrecht', p. 223.
4.   Wolff, 'Wissen um Gott', pp. 199ff.

the Jacob cycle in Genesis as to how these reports were shaped. The book of Hosea is in all probability the oldest written record we have of the Jacob stories. Nonetheless, given the compact form that they have received thanks to Hosea (and his redactors) having only reproduced exactly what was necessary in order to get the message out, we now have no possibility for reconstructing the traditions that lie behind the book of Hosea, whether they be oral or written.

Jacob is used as an example for Israel. Just as Jacob surrendered himself to Yahweh of Hosts in Bethel, so must the people come (back) to the proper cult of Yahweh. They must recognize that Yahweh's history with Jacob has significance for themselves. They should learn from Jacob. He was faithful to Yahweh, even when Yahweh showed himself to be weak, as at Penuel; and he was found by Yahweh in Bethel, just as Israel is said in other places to have been found. Jacob's path led to Yahweh in Bethel; Yahweh will help Israel to turn back so that they will (again) worship the true God. Jacob was *found*. By saying this, Hosea states that he was *chosen*. The entire pericope in Hos. 12.3-7 culminates in Hos. 12.6-7: the name of the true God, who also speaks to the people in Bethel, is emphasized. And the people are not abandoned to themselves: with the help of God, they will turn back (12.7a). The conversion, that is to say, the recognition of Yahweh as God, will then make itself manifest in that Israel executes חסד and משפט and puts its trust in God (12.7b). Precisely by means of the proper course of action, it will be seen that the people have דעת אלהים. The knowledge of how God dealt with Israel's eponymous ancestor leads forward to the attitudes embodied in חסד and משפט. The lawsuit that is proclaimed against Israel reveals itself through דעת אלהים to be a lawsuit for the purpose of conversion. Through דעת אלהים conversion is achieved, the possibility of salvation.

The goal of דעת is here explicitly Israel's salvation, just as it is implicitly in other passages in the book of Hosea. In this connection, 'implicitly' means that it is not unequivocally clear in the individual pericopes that conversion is the intention. It is obvious, however, that the conversion of the people is the ultimate purpose of the proclamation throughout the entire book of Hosea. In spite of the powerful images and the sharp condemnation of the people and their leaders, the book of Hosea nevertheless repeatedly points to Yahweh's desire that the people will accept him as God.

L. Perlitt claims that 'There were no ancient election traditions in Israel's faith, but there were, however, ancient salvation-historical traditions...'[5] He locates the passages concerning these salvation-historical traditions in the book of Amos,[6] but then adds: 'In the final analysis, however, Amos says something that is the diametrical opposite of a promising theology of election'.[7]

What Amos does not say of election theology, Hosea does say. By means of historical recollections, Hosea makes it clear that Yahweh has a claim upon Israel and that this claim is substantiated through his dealings with Israel throughout Israel's history. Again, it is this claim, that we have called the demand for exclusivity. Covenantal theology is not an ancient institution. Israel has not understood itself to be exclusively Yahweh's people from the very beginning. That they should be Yahweh's—and only Yahweh's—people is the content of the demand for exclusivity—and that is what is new here. This new way of thinking arose with the advent of eighth-century prophecy, first and foremost with Hosea.

E.W. Nicholson in *God and his People*[8] attempts to determine the mode of thought that separates the religion of Israel from that of the surrounding societies. Unlike scholars from the first half of the century, Nicholson does not take his point of departure in the assumption that Israel was totally different from the neighbouring societies from the very beginning of its existence. Like B. Lang (and with H.H. Schmid), he describes pre-prophetic religion in Israel as a common form of the ancient Near Eastern fertility religions, which is a polytheistic religion, in which Yahweh also has a place in the pantheon. Such a religion exists in order to maintain the cosmos at every level—in both nature and politics—and the cult is performed with this intention in view. The world in essence is sacred—the maintenance of the world order is assured by means of cooperation with the gods, and worship is conducted, finally, for the sake of human beings.

But, says Nicholson, Israelite henotheism and, as time went on, monotheism had a different understanding of the world, which became desacralized, and of God. When Israel should exclusively worship Yahweh, this took place 'to the greater glory of God'. The fulfilment of

---

5. Perlitt, *Bundestheologie*, p. 117; *versus*, for example, H. Wildberger, *Jahwes Eigentumsvolk*.

6. Amos 5.25; 9.7; 2.9; 3.2, Perlitt, *Bundestheologie*, p. 136.

7. Perlitt, *Bundestheologie*, p. 177, and p. 136.

8. For the following, see Nicholson, *God and his People*, ch. 10: 'The Covenant and the Distinctiveness of Israel's Faith', pp. 191-217.

Yahweh's righteousness is the nation's *raison d'être*.[9] The development
of this theology, in which the demand for exclusivity is an important
component, reaches its culmination in the Deuteronomistic covenantal
theology. But, as Wellhausen claimed,[10] this development has an
important background in the prophetic movement. The prophets did not
actually 'invent' the theology of exclusivity, for they are drawing upon
tendencies that were already present at an earlier stage in Israelite
religion. But Nicholson regards prophecy as the decisive factor in the
internal Israelite dispute about the nature of God and his relation to the
world and Israel.[11]

Hosea and the Hosean tradition play an important role in this dispute.
We have seen how Hosea shows, by using Jacob as an example, that
Israel must worship Yahweh alone in Bethel. The phrase 'Yahweh, the
God of Hosts, Yahweh is his name' (Hos. 12.6) underscores that it is
precisely this God and no other that is at issue. The Jacob pericope in
Hos. 12.13-14 emphasizes the interdependence between God and the
people, and, at the same time, by means of its structure refers to the
other traditions of the past in which Yahweh's care for his people is a
recurrent theme. Further, we have seen how Hosea employs older
motifs and traditions, both 'historical' and 'theological', and that it is this
material that is characterized as דעת אלהים. This knowledge should and
ought to be the people's possession, and Hosea can also presuppose that
certain portions of it are known. We have repeatedly seen it demonstrated that this was the case.

But it is Hosea's claim that what is not known to Israel is the demand
that is inherent in Yahweh's historical dealings with his people, the
demand for exclusive worship of Yahweh. When Hosea in 4.4-6 says to
the priests that they are guilty in the destruction of the people because
the people lack knowledge, the knowledge mentioned is the knowledge
of Yahweh's demand for exclusivity, not simply teaching of 'Scripture'.
Something similar can be seen in 6.1-6. The people's understanding of
Yahweh is different from that which Hosea regards as being the only
true understanding of Yahweh. For the people, Yahweh is the maintainer
of the cosmos, who, albeit he has wounded, will also heal. The people are

9. Nicholson, *God and his People*, p. 201.
10. Nicholson's book not only marks a return to Wellhausen, but the book
further develops Wellhausen's basic insight with attention given to an entire century's
developments within the areas of the history of religions and the sociology of religion.
11. Nicholson, *God and his People*, p. 201.

in a sense pious and believing, but their faith is without reality, without genuine substance and consistency, 'like the morning cloud, like the dew that goes away early' (6.4b). They do not know Yahweh's demand. His punishment is the words of judgment that Hosea speaks to them. What he requires is recognition of his demand for exclusivity, which they should receive with חסד, not with sacrifices (6.6). Although I am unable to regard Hos. 6.4-10 as having originally been of one piece,[12] it does therefore make good sense that 6.7 with the accusation of a breach of covenant follows after the demand for חסד and דעת אלהים in 6.6.[13] For Hosea the covenant has not become a *theologumenon* as in the Deuteronomistic circle; but it is one of Hosea's images for the proper relationship to God, as this relationship ought to be.

What Hosea does emphasize time after time in his 'historical' retrospections is that Israel is chosen. The finding is election; the call is an election; the education of the fair heifer is election. But not an election to a life in passive retreat. The election means that Israel must serve and worship Yahweh alone. This is most clear in 13.4. Yahweh declares himself to be the one who alone[14] has been Israel's God from the very beginning. The same message comes clearly to view in 10.11-12. Ephraim was trained beforehand, but was chosen to serve Yahweh with צדקה and חסד. That Yahweh has a demand upon Israel is also quite clear in that portion of the book of Hosea that has been virtually undealt with in this study, namely Hosea 1–3. Here it is the marital image, as is well-known, that is the dominating image in the demand for exclusivity—and quite naturally. The ancient Near Eastern marital institution was an excellent depiction of the relationship between a sovereign deity and the people of his possession, who live only for the sake of his glory. The images in Hosea 2 of a people, exclusively dependent upon Yahweh's creative power, are supplemented by recollections from their common history, again from the call out of Egypt. Before the lawsuit against the faithless, ignorant wife, we find the threefold denial of her children (Hos. 1), which reaches its climax in the anti-thesis of the covenant formulary: 'You are not my people, and I am not your God' (Hos. 1.9).

This is the Yahweh-alone theology that Hosea proclaims. With the

---

12. *Pace*, among others, Nicholson, *God and his People*, p. 180.

13. It can here be seen that redactional work does not always destroy the original intention.

14. Note that it is not a question of a *monotheistic* declaration. The existence of other gods is not denied.

religio-historical presentation in mind, one could be tempted to accuse him of unfairness. But Hosea sees Yahweh's election of the people as being so closely connected with his demand for exclusivity that the story of this election in itself ought to have made this demand clear to the people. The people that have lived together with Yahweh ought to have known better than to have worshipped other gods. If the people had been in possession of the proper דעת אלהים, then they would have shown חסד towards Yahweh and served him לצדקה (Hos. 10.12).

The proclamation of the demand for exclusivity was a renewal of Israelite religion's innermost content. This understanding supports the claim that Hosea was indeed not opposed to the cult and was not in principle opposed to the priesthood. Precisely because Hosea claims that what he says is not anything new, but from time immemorial has been the true content of Yahweh faith, he does not condemn the cult and cultic places as such, but only the present cult. And for precisely this reason there is no oppositional relationship in principle between Hosea and the priesthood, although the present priesthood must be rejected. The role that Hosea himself plays is priestly;[15] he proclaims true knowledge of God, and he does so by the use of cultic language, just as we have previously seen, for example in Hos. 6.1-6; 10.11-13a.

Yahweh's history with Israel has been characterized by the fact that the people have lacked דעת אלהים. Hosea must set forth the judgment: Yahweh will draw back so that they can no longer find him; he will no longer love them, and war and destruction will be upon them. But this is not the final outcome of Yahweh's history with his people. As over against the Deuteronomistic History, the book of Hosea is not primarily an explanation that follows after the execution of the judgment. The book of Hosea speaks before the judgment, and with those passages in mind where Yahweh refuses to punish his people in spite of their guilt, the book of Hosea must be perceived as a warning and not as an inevitable oracle of doom. Yahweh's anger is not the last word; as it is stated in Hos. 11.8-9, and correspondingly in Hosea 14, Yahweh himself will heal their apostasy (14.5; and cf. 12.3-7). The intention is that the people will return to that situation in which they stood before Yahweh in the beginning (2.16-17, 18-20 [MT]). We see two pictures of the possibility of restoration in these examples: Yahweh heals and punishes. But the result is the same: Israel will 'respond, as in the days of her youth' (Hos. 2.17).

15. Cf. Zimmerli, *Gottesrecht*, pp. 220, 228.

BIBLIOGRAPHY

Ackroyd, P.R., 'Hosea and Jacob', *VT* 13 (1963), pp. 245-59.

Ahlström, G.W., *Who were the Israelites?* (Winona Lake, IN: Eisenbrauns, 1986).

Alt, A., 'Hosea 5,8–6,6. Ein Krieg und seine Folgen in prophetischer Beleuchtung', *NKZ* 30 (1919), pp. 537-68 (= *KS*, II [Munich: C.H. Beck, 1953] pp. 163-87).

—'Die Heimat des Deuteronomiums', *KS*, II (Munich: C.H. Beck, 1953), pp. 250-75.

Aurelius, E., *Der Fürbitter Israels: Eine Studie zum Mosebild im Alten Testament* (ConBOT 27; Stockholm: Almquist & Wiksell International, 1988).

Bach, R., 'Die Erwählung Israels in der Wüste' (Dissertation; Bonn 1952).

Balz-Cochois, H., *Gomer: Der Höhenkult Israels im Selbstverständnis der Volksfrömmigkeit. Untersuchungen zu Hosea 4,1–5,7* (Europäische Hochschulschriften, Reihe XXIII, Bd 191; Frankfurt a.M: Lang, 1982).

Barth, C., 'Zur Bedeutung der Wüstentradition' (VTSup 15; Leiden: E.J. Brill, 1966), pp. 14-23.

Barton, J., *Reading the Old Testament: Method in Biblical Study* (London: Darton, Longman & Todd, 1984).

Baudissin, W.W. Graf, *Adonis und Esmun: Eine Untersuchung zur Geschichte des Glaubens an Auferstehungsgötter und an Heilgötter* (Leipzig: Hinrichs, 1911).

Baumann, E., '"Wissen um Gott" bei Hosea als Urform von Theologie?', *EvT* 15 (1955), pp. 416-25.

—'Das Lied Moses (Dt. XXXII 1-43) auf seine gedankliche Geschlossenheit untersucht', *VT* 6 (1956), pp. 414-24.

Bentzen, A., *Die josianische Reform und ihre Voraussetzungen* (Copenhagen: P. Haase & søn, 1926).

—'The Weeping of Jacob, Hos XII$_{5a}$', *VT* 1 (1951), pp. 58-59.

Blum, E., *Die Komposition der Vätergeschichte* (WMANT 57; Neukirchen–Vluyn: Neukirchener Verlag, 1984).

Boer, P.A.H. de, 'Genesis XXXII$_{23-33}$. Some Remarks on Composition and Character of the Story', *NedTT's* 1 (1946–47), pp. 149-63.

Böhmer, S., *Heimkehr und neuer Bund: Studien zu Jeremia 30–31* (Göttingen: Vandenhoeck & Ruprecht, 1976).

Carroll, R.P., *Jeremiah: A Commentary* (OTL; London: SCM Press, 1986).

Childs, B.S., *Introduction to the Old Testament as Scripture* (London: SCM Press, 1979).

Clements, R.E., *Prophecy and Tradition* (Oxford: Basil Blackwell, 1975).

Clines, D.J.A., 'Hosea 2: Structure and Interpretation', in E.A. Livingstone (ed.), *Studia Biblica 1978*, I (JSOTSup 11; Sheffield: JSOT Press, 1979), pp. 83-103.

Cross, F.M., *Canaanite Myth and Hebrew Epic: Essays in the History of the Religion of Israel* (Cambridge, MA: Harvard University Press, 1973).

Crüsemann, F., *Bewahrung der Freiheit: Das Thema des Dekalogs in Sozialge-schichtlicher Perspektive* (KT 78; Munich: Chr. Kaiser, 1983).

Day, J., 'Pre-Deuteronomic Allusions to the Covenant in Hosea and Psalm LXXVIII', *VT* 36 (1986), pp. 1-12.

Diebner, B.J., '"Es lässt sich nicht beweisen, Tatsache aber ist…" Sprachfigur statt Methode in der kritischen Erforschung des AT', *DBAT* 18 (1984), pp. 138-46.

—'Forschungsgeschichtliche Einführung', in Friis, *Die Bedingungen für die Errichtung des Davidischen Reichs in Israel und seiner Umwelt* (*q.v.*), pp. 217-41.

Dijk-Hemmes, F. van, 'The Metaphorization of Woman in Prophetic Speech: An Analysis of Ezekiel 23' (unpublished, short communication, IOSOT Congress, Leuven, August 1989).

Duhm, B., *Jeremia* (KHCAT 11; Tübingen: J.C.B. Mohr [Paul Siebeck], 1901).

Edelman, D. (ed.), *Toward a Consensus on the Emergence of Israel in Canaan: Papers Read at the SBL/ASOR Hebrew Bible, History and Archaeology Section* (AAR/SBL Annual Meeting, New Orleans, 1990), *SJOT* 5 (1991), pp. 1-116.

Emmerson, G.I., *Hosea: An Israelite Prophet in Judean Perspective* (JSOTSup 28; Sheffield: JSOT Press, 1984).

Engnell, I., *Gamla Testamentet: En traditionshistorisk inledning*, I (Stockholm: Svenska Kyrkans Diakonistyrelse, 1945).

—'Betel', *SBU*, I (ed. I. Engnell, Stockholm: Nordiska Uppslagsböcker, 2nd edn, 1962), col, 251-52.

Eslinger, L.M., 'Hosea 12.5a and Genesis 32.29: A Study in Inner-Biblical Exegesis', *JSOT* 18 (1980), pp. 91-99.

Finkelstein, I., *The Archaeology of the Israelite Settlement* (Jerusalem: Israel Exploration Society, 1988).

Fishbane, M., *Biblical Interpretation in Ancient Israel* (Oxford: Clarendon, 1985).

Fohrer, G., 'Umkehr und Erlösung beim Propheten Hosea', *TZ* 11 (1955), pp. 161-85.

Francisco, C.T., 'Evil and Suffering in the Book of Hosea', *SWJT* 5 (1962), pp. 33-41.

Friis, H., 'Ein neues Paradigma für die Erforschung der Vorgeschichte Israels?', *DBAT* 19 (1984), pp. 3-22.

—*Die Bedingungen für die Errichtung des Davidischen Reichs in Israel und seiner Umwelt* (BDBAT 6; Heidelberg: private edition, 1986).

Gese, H., 'Kleine Beiträge zum Verständnis des Amosbuches', *VT* 12 (1962), pp. 417-38.

—'Bemerkungen zur Sinaitradition', *ZAW* 79 (1967), pp. 137-154 (= *Vom Sinai zum Zion* [Alttestamentliche Beiträge zur biblischen Theologie; Munich: Chr. Kaiser, 1974], pp. 31-48).

—'Jacob und Mose: Hosea 12,3-14 als einheitlicher Text', in J.W. van Henten *et al.* (eds.), *Tradition and Reinterpretation in Jewish and Early Christian Literature* (FS J.C.H. Lebram; Studia Post-Biblica 36; Leiden: E.J. Brill, 1986), pp. 38-47.

Ginsberg, H.L., 'Hosea's Ephraim, More Fool Than Knave: A New Interpretation of Hosea 12.1-14', *JBL* 80 (1961), pp. 339-47.

Glueck, N., *Das Wort hesed im alttestamentlichen Sprachgebrauche als menschliche und göttliche gemeinschaftsgemässe Verhaltungsweise* (BZAW 47; Giessen: Alfred Töpelmann, 1927).

Good, E.M., 'The Composition of Hosea', *SEÅ* 31 (1966), pp. 21-63.

—'Hosea 5,8–6,6: An Alternative to Alt', *JBL* 85 (1966), pp. 273-86.

—'Hosea and the Jacob Tradition', *VT* 16 (1966), pp. 137-51.

Gottlieb, H., 'Den tærskende kvie—Mi 4,11-13', *DTT* 26 (1963), pp. 167-71.

Gottwald, N.K., *The Tribes of Yahweh: A Sociology of the Religion of Liberated Israel, 1250–1050 BCE* (Maryknoll: Orbis, 1979).

Gunkel, H., *Genesis* (Göttingen: Vandenhoeck & Ruprecht, 8th edn, 1969).

Gunneweg, A.H.J., *Leviten und Priester* (Göttingen: Vandenhoeck & Ruprecht, 1965).

Hammershaimb, E., *Some Aspects of Old Testament Prophecy from Isaiah to Malachi* (Copenhagen: Rosenkilde og Bagger, 1966).

Hentschke, R., *Die Stellung der vorexilischen Schriftpropheten zum Kultus* (BZAW 75; Berlin: Alfred Töpelmann, 1957).

Herrmann, S., *Die prophetische Heilserwartungen im Alten Testament: Ursprung und Gestaltwandel* (BWANT 5. Folge, Heft 5; Stuttgart: W. Kohlhammer, 1965).

—*Geschichte Israels in alttestamentlicher Zeit* (Munich: Chr. Kaiser, 2nd rev. edn, 1980) (ET: *A History of Israel in Old Testament Times* (Revised and Enlarged Edition; trans. John Bowden; Philadelphia: Westminster Press, 1981]).

Hidal, S., 'Reflections on Deuteronomy 32', *ASTI*, XI (1977–78), pp. 15-21.

Holt, E.K., (= Kragelund, E.), 'Fra profeti til prædiken: Jeremias'og Jeremiasbogens forhold til den deuteronomistiske tradition i lyset af nyere forskning' (unpublished prize paper, Aarhus Universitet, 1982/83).

—'דעת אלהים und חסד im Buche Hosea', *SJOT* 1 (1987), pp. 87-103.

—'The Chicken and the Egg—Or: Was Jeremiah a Member of the Deuteronomist Party?', *JSOT* 44 (1989), pp. 109-22.

Horst, F., *Das Privilegrecht Jahwes: Rechtsgeschichtliche Untersuchungen zum Deuteronomium* (FRLANT 45 [NF 28]; Göttingen: Vandenhoeck & Ruprecht, 1930) (= F. Horst, *Gottes Recht: Gesammelte Studien zum Recht im Alten Testament* [TB 12; Munich: Chr. Kaiser, 1961], pp. 17-154).

Hossfeld, F.L., *Der Dekalog: Seine späten Fassungen, die originale Komposition und seine Vorstufen* (OBO 45; Freiburg: Universitätsverlag, 1982).

Hvidberg, F.F., *Weeping and Laughter in the Old Testament: A Study of Canaanite-Israelite Religion* (posthumously ed. F. Løkkegaard; Leiden: E.J. Brill, 1961).

Hvidberg-Hansen, O., 'Die Vernichtung des goldenen Kalbes und die ugaritische Ernteritus. Der rituelle Hintergrund für Exod. 32,20 und andere alttestamentliche Berichte über die Vernichtung von Götterbildern', *AcOr* (L) 33 (1971), pp. 5-46.

Jacob, E., 'Der Prophet Hosea und die Geschichte', *EvT* 24 (1964), pp. 281-90.

Jensen, H.J.L., 'Mytebegrebet i den historisk-kritiske og i den strukturalistiske forskning', *DTT* 47 (1984), pp. 1-19.

—'Den strukturelle myteanalyse—og Det gamle Testamente', in B. Otzen, H. Gottlieb, K. Jeppesen and H.J.L. Jensen, *Myter i Det gamle Testamente* (Frederiksberg: Anis, 2nd edn, 1990), pp. 153-216.

Jensen, J., *The Use of tôrâ by Isaiah: His Debate with the Wisdom Tradition* (CBQMS 3; Washington DC: The Catholic Biblical Association of America, 1973).

Jeppesen, K., *Græder ikke saa saare: Studier i Mikabogens sigte*, I-II (Aarhus: Aarhus Universitetsforlag, 1987).

—'Myth in the Prophetic Literature', in B. Otzen, H. Gottlieb and K. Jeppesen, *Myths in the Old Testament* (London: SCM Press, 1980), pp. 94-123.

Jeppesen, K., and B. Otzen (eds.), *The Productions of Time: Tradition History in Old Testament Scholarship* (Sheffield: The Almond Press, 1984).

Jepsen, A., 'Gnade und Barmherzigkeit im Alten Testament', *KD* 7 (1961), pp. 261-71.

—'צדק und צדקה im Alten Testament', in H. Graf Reventlow (ed.), *Gottes Wort und Gottes Land* (FS H.-W. Hertzberg; Göttingen: Vandenhoeck & Ruprecht, 1965), pp. 78-89.

Jeremias, J., 'Hosea 4–7. Beobachtungen zur Komposition des Buches Hosea', in A.H.J. Gunneweg and O. Kaiser (eds.), *Textgemäss: Aufsätze und Beiträge zur Hermeneutik des Alten Testaments* (FS E. Würthwein; Göttingen: Vandenhoeck & Ruprecht, 1979), pp. 47-58.

—*Der Prophet Hosea* (ATD 24/1; Göttingen: Vandenhoeck & Ruprecht, 1983).

Junker, H., 'Textkritische, formkritische und traditionsgeschichtliche Untersuchungen zu Os 4,1-10', *BZ* NF 4 (1960), pp. 165-73.

Justi, C.W. (ed.), *Blumen althebraischer Dichtkunst* (Giessen, 1809).

Kaiser, W., Jr, 'Inner Biblical Exegesis as a Model for Bridging the "Then" and "Now" Gap: Hosea 12,1-6', *JETS* 28 (1985), pp. 33-46.

Kapelrud, A.S., *Baal in the Ras Shamra Texts* (Copenhagen: G.E.C. Gad, 1952).

—*The Violent Goddess: Anat in the Ras Shamra Texts* (Oslo: Universitetsforlaget, 1969).

Kinet, D., *Ba'al und Jahwe: Ein Beitrag zur Theologie des Hoseabuches* (Europäische Hochschulschriften, Reihe XXIII, Bd 87; Frankfurt a.M.: Lang, 1977).

Koch, K., 'Ṣdq im Alten Testament: Eine traditionsgeschichtliche Untersuchung' (Dissertation, Heidelberg, 1953).

—'Gibt es ein Vergeltungsdogma im Alten Testament?', *ZTK* 52 (1955), pp. 1-42 (= K. Koch, [ed.], *Um das Prinzip der Vergeltung in Religion und Recht des Alten Testaments* [Darmstadt: Wissenschaftliche Buchgesellschaft, 1972], pp. 130-80).

—'צדק ṣdq gemeinschaftstreu/heilvoll sein', *THAT*, II, cols. 507-30.

Kümpel, R., 'Die Berufung Israels: Ein Beitrag zu Theologie des Hosea' (Dissertation, Bonn, 1973).

Lang, B. (ed.), *Der einzige Gott: Die Geburt des biblischen Monotheismus* (Munich: Kösel, 1981).

—'Die Jahwe-allein-Bewegung', in Lang (ed.), *Der einzige Gott: Die Geburt des biblischen Monotheismus (q.v.)*, pp. 47-83.

—*Monotheism and the Prophetic Minority: An Essay in Biblical History and Sociology* (SWBA 1; Sheffield: The Almond Press, 1983).

Lehming, S., 'Versuch zu Ex XXXII', *VT* 10 (1960), pp. 16-50.

Lemche, N.P., *Early Israel: Anthropological and Historical Studies on the Israelite Society before the Monarchy* (VTSup 37; Leiden: E.J. Brill, 1985).

—'Kan man knuse jern, jern fra nord, og bronze?', in K. Jeppesen and J. Strange, *Skriv synet tyde ligt pa° tavler! Omproblemerne ved en ny bibeloversæHelse.* (Copenhagen: Gad, 1988), pp. 54-71.

—*Ancient Israel: A New History of Israelite Society* (The Biblical Seminar, 5; Sheffield: JSOT Press, 1988).

—'The Development of the Israelite Religion in Light of Recent Studies on the Early History of Israel', in J.A. Emerton (ed.), *Congress Volume, Leuven 1989* (VTSup 43; Leiden: E.J. Brill, 1991), pp. 97-115.

—*The Canaanites and their Land* (JSOTSup 110; Sheffield: JSOT Press, 1991).

Levin, C., *Die Verheissung des neuen Bundes in ihrem theologiegeschichtlichen Zusammenhang ausgelegt* (FRLANT 137; Göttingen: Vandenhoeck & Ruprecht, 1985).

Lindblom, J., *Prophecy in Ancient Israel* (Oxford: Basil Blackwell, 1962).

Lohfink, N., SJ, 'Zu Text und Form von Os 4,4-6', *Bib* 42 (1961), pp. 303-32.

—'Hate and Love in Hosea 9,15', *CBQ* 25 (1963), p. 417.

McKane, W., *Jeremiah*, I (ICC; Edinburg: T. & T. Clark, 1986).

Marti, K., *Das Dodekapropheton* (KHCAT 13; Tübingen: Mohr [Paul Siebeck], 1904).

May, H.G., 'The Fertility Cult in Hosea', *AJSL* 48 (1932), pp. 73-98.

Mayes, A.D.H., *Deuteronomy* (NCB; Greenwood, SC: Attic Press, 1979).

Mays, J.L., *Hosea: A Commentary* (OTL; London: SCM Press, 1969).

Mettinger, T.N.D., 'YHWH SABAOTH—The Heavenly King on the Cherubim Throne', in T. Ishida (ed.), *Studies in the Period of David and Solomon and other Essays: Papers Read at the International Symposium for Biblical Studies, Tokyo, 5-7 December, 1979* (Tokyo: Yamakawa-Shuppansa, 1982), pp. 109-38.

Miller, J.M., and J.H. Hayes, *A History of Ancient Israel and Judah* (Philadelphia: Westminster Press, 1986).

Mogensen, B., '$s^e daqa$ in the Scandinavian and German Research Traditions', in Jeppesen and Otzen (eds.), *The Productions of Time: Tradition History in Old Testament Scholarship* (*q.v.*), pp. 67-80.

Mowinckel, S., *Zur Komposition des Buches Jeremia* (Videnskapsselskapets Skrifter II, Hist. filos. Klasse, 1913, No. 5; Kristiania: Jacob Dybwad, 1914).

—*The Psalms in Israel's Worship*, I, II (trans. D.R. Ap-Thomas; Oxford: Basil Blackwell, 1962).

Naumann, T., *Hoseas Erben: Strukturen der Nachinterpretatition im Buch Hosea* (BWANT; Köln: W. Kohlhammer Verlag, 1991).

Neef, H.-D., *Die Heilstraditionen Israels in der Verkündigung des Propheten Hosea* (BZAW 169; Berlin: Walter de Gruyter, 1987).

Nicholson, E.W., *God and his People: Covenant and Theology in the Old Testament* (Oxford: Clarendon Press, 1986).

Nielsen, E., *Oral Tradition: A Modern Problem in Old Testament Introduction* (SBT; London: SCM Press, 1954).

—*Shechem: A Traditio-Historical Investigation* (Copenhagen: G.E.C. Gad, 1955).

—'The Levites in Ancient Israel', *ASTI* 3 (1964), pp. 16-27 (= S. Holm-Nielsen *et al.* [eds.], *Law, History and Tradition* [FS E. Nielsen; Copenhagen: G.E.C. Gad, 1983], pp. 71-81).

—'Historical Perspectives and Geographical Horizons. On the Question of North-Israelite Elements in Deuteronomy', *ASTI* 11 (1977–78), pp. 77-89 (= S. Holm-Nielsen *et al.* (eds.), *Law, History and Tradition* [FS E. Nielsen; Copenhagen: G.E.C. Gad, 1983], pp. 82-93).

Nielsen, K., 'Profeternes opgør med kulten. Licentiatforelæsning 30.9.1976', *DTT* 39 (1976), pp. 217-30.

—*Yahweh as Prosecutor and Judge: An Investigation of the Prophetic Lawsuit (Rîb-Pattern)* (JSOTSup 9; Sheffield: JSOT Press, 1978).

—*There is Hope for a Tree: The Tree as Metaphor in Isaiah* (trans. C. and F. Crowley; JSOTSup 65; Sheffield: JSOT Press, 1989) (= *For et træ er der håb: Om træet som metafor i Jes 1–39* [Copenhagen: G.E.C. Gad, 1985]).

Nissinen, M., *Prophetie, Redaktion und Fortschreibung im Hoseabuch: Studien zum Werdegang eines Prophetenbuches im Lichte von Hos 4 und 11* (AOAT 231; Neukirchen-Vluyn: Neukirchener Verlag, 1991).

Noth, M., *Überlieferungsgeschichtliche Studien. I. Die sammelnden und bearbeitenden Geschichtswerke im Alten Testament* (Tübingen: Max Niemeyer, 1943).

—*Überlieferungsgeschichte des Pentateuch* (Stuttgart: W. Kohlhammer, 1948).

—*Geschichte Israels* (Göttingen: Vandenhoeck und Ruprecht, 2nd edn, 1954).

Nowack, W., *Die kleinen Propheten* (HK III/4; Göttingen: Vandenhoeck & Ruprecht, 3rd edn, 1922).

Nyberg, H.S., *Studien zum Hoseabuche* (UUÅ [1935] 6; Uppsala: A.B. Lundequistska Bokhandeln, 1935).

Pedersen, J., *Israel: Its Life and Culture*, I-IV[4] (London, 1959) (trans. A. Møller from *Israel*. *I-II Sjæleliv og Samfundsliv* [Copenhagen, 1920], *III-IV Hellighed og Guddommelighed* [Copenhagen, 1934]).

Perlitt, L., *Bundestheologie im Alten Testament* (WMANT 36; Neukirchen-Vluyn: Neukirchener Verlag, 1969).

Petersen, D.L., *The Roles of Israel's Prophets* (JSOTSup 17; Sheffield: JSOT Press, 1981).

Rad, G. von, 'Die levitische Predigt in den Büchern der Chronik', in *Festschrift O. Procksch* (Leipzig: A. Deichert, 1934), pp. 113-24 (= *Gesammelte Studien zum Alten Testament* [TB 8; Munich: Chr. Kaiser Verlag, 1961], pp. 248-61).

—*Das Formgeschichtliche Problem des Hexateuch* (BWANT 4. Folge, Heft 26; Stuttgart: W. Kohlhammer, 1938) (= *Gesammelte Studien zum Alten Testament* [TB 8; Munich: Chr. Kaiser Verlag, 1961], pp. 9-86).

—*Deuteronomiumstudien* (Göttingen: Vandenhoeck & Ruprecht, 1948). (ET??)

—*Das fünfte Buch Mose—Deuteronomium* (ATD 8; Göttingen: Vandenhoeck & Ruprecht, 2nd edn, 1968).

—*Das erste Buch Mose—Genesis* (ATD 2/4; Göttingen: Vandenhoeck & Ruprecht, 9th rev. edn, 1976).

—*Theologie des Alten Testaments. I. Die Theologie der Geschichtliche Überlieferungen Israels* (Munich: Chr. Kaiser Verlag, 8th edn, 1982).

Reiterer, F.V., *Gerechtigkeit als Heil: צדק bei Deuterojesaja. Aussage und Vergleich mit der alttestamentlischen Tradition* (Graz: Akademische Druck und Verlagsanstalt, 1976).

Rendtorff, R., *Das Überlieferungsgeschichtliche Problem des Pentateuch* (BZAW 147; Berlin: Alfred Töpelmann, 1977).

—'Zur Komposition des Buches Jesaja', *VT* 34 (1984), pp. 295-320.

Robinson, H.W., 'The Hebrew Concept of Corporate Personality', in P. Volz *et al.* (eds.), *Werden und Wesen des Alten Testaments* (BZAW 66; Berlin: Alfred Töpelmann, 1936), pp. 49-62.

Rose, M., *Der Ausschliesslichkeitsanspruch Jahwes: Deuteronomistische Schultheologie und die Volksfrömmigkeit in der späten Königszeit* (BWANT 6. Folge, Heft 6; Stuttgart: W. Kohlhammer, 1975).

Roth, W.M.W., 'The Numerical Sequence x/x+1 in the Old Testament', *VT* 12 (1962), pp. 300-11.

Rudolph, W., *Hosea* (KAT 13/1; Gütersloh: Gütersloher Verlagshaus Gerd Mohn, 1966).

Schlisske, W., *Gottessöhne und Gottessohn im Alten Testament: Phasen der Entmythisierung im Alten Testament* (BWANT 5. Folge, Heft 17; Stuttgart: W. Kohlhammer Verlag, 1973).

Schmid, H., *Die Gestalt des Mose: Probleme alttestamentlicher Forschung unter Berücksichtigung der Pentateuchkrise* (Erträge der Forschung 237; Darmstadt: Wissenschaftliche Buchgesellschaft, 1986).

Schmid, H.H., *Gerechtigkeit als Weltordnung: Hintergrund und Geschichte des alttestamentlichen Gerechtigkeitsbegriffes* (Tübingen: J.C.B. Mohr, 1968).

—*Der sogenannte Jahwist: Beobachtungen und Fragen zur Pentateuchforschung* (Zürich: Theologischer Verlag, 1976).

Schmidt, H., 'Hosea 6,1-6', in A. Jirku (ed.), *Beiträge zur Religionsgeschichte und Archäologie Palästinas* (FS E. Sellin; Leipzig: A. Deichert, 1927), pp. 111-26.

Schmidt, W.H., 'Die deuteronomistische Redaktion des Amosbuches. Zu den theologischen Unterschieden zwischen dem Prophetenwort und seinem Sammler', *ZAW* 77 (1965), pp. 168-93.

—'"Suchet den Herrn, so werdet Ihr leben". Exegetische Notizen zum Thema "Gott suchen" in der Prophetie', in C.J. Bleeker *et al.* (eds.), *Ex Orbe Religionum* (FS G. Widengren; Leiden: E.J. Brill, 1972), pp. 127-40.

Schmitt, G., 'Der Ursprung des Levitentums', *ZAW* 94 (1982), pp. 575-99.

Schottroff, W., 'Jeremia 2,1-3: Erwägungen zur Methode der Prophetenexegese', *ZTK* 67 (1970), pp. 263-94.

Schreiner, J., 'עול 'awæl', *ThWAT*, V, cols. 1135-44.

Sellin, E., *Das Zwölfprophetenbuch* (KAT 12; Leipzig, 3rd edn, 1929 [1922]).

Selms, A. van, 'Temporary Henotheism', in M.A. Beek *et al.* (eds.), *Symbolae Biblicae et Mesopotamicae* (FS F.M.T. de Liagre Böhl; Leiden: Brill, 1973), pp. 341-48.

Smith, M., *Palestinian Parties and Politics That Shaped the Old Testament* (London: SCM Press, 1971).

Stolz, F., *Strukturen und Figuren im Kult von Jerusalem: Studien zur altorientalischen, Vor- und Frühisraelitischen Religion* (BZAW 118; Berlin: Töpelmann, 1970).

Stuart, D., *Hosea—Jonah* (WBC 31; Waco, TX: Word Books, 1987).

Sundén, H., *Die Religion und die Rollen: Eine psychologische Untersuchung der Frömmigkeit* (Berlin: Alfred Töpelmann, 1966).

Sweeney, M.A., *Isaiah 1–4 and the Post-Exilic Understanding of the Isaianic Tradition* (BZAW 171; Berlin: Alfred Töpelmann, 1988).

Thiel, W., *Die deuteronomistische Redaktion von Jeremia 1–25* (WMANT 41; Neukirchen–Vluyn: Neukirchener Verlag, 1973).

Van Seters, J., *Abraham in History and Tradition* (New Haven: Yale University Press, 1975).

—'The Religion of the Patriarchs in Genesis', *Bib* 61 (1980), pp. 220-33.

Vollmer, J., *Geschichtliche Rückblicke und Motive in der Prophetie des Amos, Hosea und Jesaja* (BZAW 119; Berlin: Walter de Gruyter, 1971).

Volz, P., 'Die radikale Ablehnung der Kultreligion durch die alttestamentlichen Propheten', *ZST* 14 (1937), pp. 63-85.

Vriezen, T. C., 'La Tradition de Jacob dans Osée XII', *OTS* 1 (1942), pp. 64-78.

Weinfeld, M., *Deuteronomy and the Deuteronomic School* (Oxford: Oxford University Press, 1972).

Weiser, A., *Das Buch der zwölf kleinen Propheten. I. Die Propheten Hosea, Joel, Amos, Obadja, Jona, Micha* (ATD 24; Göttingen: Vandenhoeck & Ruprecht, 6th edn, 1974).

—*Die Psalmen* (ATD 14/15; Göttingen: Vandenhoeck & Ruprecht, 9th edn, 1979).

Wellhausen, J., *Die kleinen Propheten: Übersetzt und erklärt* (Berlin: de Gruyter, 4th edn, 1963).

—*Prolegomena zur Geschichte Israels* (Berlin: Georg Reimer, 4th edn, 1895).

Westermann, C., 'Die Begriffe für Fragen und Suchen im Alten Testament', *KD* 6 (1960), pp. 2-30.

—*Genesis* (BKAT I/1-3; Göttingen: Vandenhoeck & Ruprecht, 1974, 1981, 1982).

154 *Hosea and History*

Whitelam, K.W., 'Between History and Literature: The Social Production of Israel's Traditions of Origin', *SJOT* 5 (1991), pp. 60-74.

Wildberger, H., *Jahwes Eigentumsvolk: Eine Studie zur Traditionsgeschichte und Theologie des Erwählungsgedankens* (ATANT 37; Zürich: Zwingli Verlag, 1960).

Willi-Plein, I., *Vorformen der Schriftexegese innerhalb des Alten Testaments: Untersuchungen zum literarischen Werden der auf Amos, Hosea und Micha zurückgehenden Bücher im hebräischen Zwölfprophetenbuch* (BZAW 123; Berlin: Walter de Gruyter, 1971).

Winther, P., 'Der Begriff "Söhne Gottes" im Moselied Dt. 32,1-43', *ZAW* 67 (1955), pp. 40-48.

Wolff, H.W., *Hosea* (Hermeneia; Philadelphia: Fortress Press, 1974 [1965]) (ET G. Stansell from *Dodekapropheton*. I. *Hosea* [BKAT XIV/1; Neukirchen–Vluyn: Neukirchener Verlag]).

—'Hoseas geistige Heimat', *TLZ* 81 (1956), cols. 83-94 (= H.W. Wolff, *Gesammelte Studien zum Alten Testament* [TB 22; Munich: Chr. Kaiser, 1964], pp. 232-50).

—'"Wissen um Gott" bei Hosea als Urform von Theologie', *EvT* 12 (1952–53), pp. 533-54 (= *Gesammelte Studien zum Alten Testament* [TB 22; Munich: Chr. Kaiser, 1964], pp. 182-205).

Wright, G.E., 'The Lawsuit of God: A Form-Critical Study of Deuteronomy 32', in B. Anderson and W. Harrelson (eds.), *Israel's Prophetic Heritage* (FS J. Muilenberg; London: SCM Press, 1962), pp. 26-67.

Würthwein, E., 'Kultpolemik oder Kultbescheid?', in E. Würthwein and O. Kaiser (eds.), *Tradition und Situation: Studien zur alttestamentlichen Prophetie* (FS A. Weiser; Göttingen: Vandenhoeck & Ruprecht, 1963), pp. 115-31.

—'Zur Komposition von 1 Reg 22.1-38', in F. Maass (ed.), *Das ferne und nahe Wort* (FS L. Rost; Berlin, 1967), pp. 245-54.

Yee, G.A., *Composition and Tradition in the Book of Hosea: A Redaction Critical Investigation* (SBLDS 102; Atlanta, GA: Scholars Press, 1987).

Zimmerli, W., *Ezechiel* (BKAT XIII/1-2; Neukirchen: Neukirchener Verlag, 1969).

—'Das Gottesrecht bei den Propheten Amos, Hosea und Jesaja', in R. Albertz *et al.* (eds.), *Werden und Wirken des Alten Testaments* (FS C. Westermann; Neukirchen–Vluyn: Neukirchener Verlag, 1980), pp. 216-35.

—'Ich bin Jahwe', in *Geschichte und Altes Testament: Aufsätze von W.F. Albright et al.* (FS A. Alt; BHT 16; Tübingen: J.C.B. Mohr [Paul Siebeck], 1953), pp. 179-208 (= W. Zimmerli, *Gottes Offenbarung: Gesammelte Aufsätze zum Alten Testament* [Munich: Chr. Kaiser, 1963], pp. 11-40).

—'χάρις', *TWNT*, IX, pp. 366-77.

INDEXES

INDEX OF BIBLICAL REFERENCES